The Church Has
Left the Building

The Church Has Left the Building

Faith, Parish, and Ministry in the Twenty-First Century

EDITORS

Michael Plekon
Maria Gwyn McDowell
Elizabeth Schroeder

FOREWORD BY

John McGuckin

 CASCADE *Books* · Eugene, Oregon

THE CHURCH HAS LEFT THE BUILDING
Faith, Parish, and Ministry in the Twenty-first Century

Cascade Books
An Imprint of Wipf and Stock Publishers
199 W. 8th Ave., Suite 3
Eugene, OR 97401

www.wipfandstock.com

PAPERBACK ISBN: 978-1-4982-3956-1
HARDCOVER ISBN: 978-1-4982-3958-5
EBOOK ISBN: 978-1-4982-3957-8

Cataloguing-in-Publication data:

Names: Plekon, Michael, 1948– | McDowell, Maria | Schroeder, Elizabeth | McGuckin, John H.

Title: The church has left the building : faith, parish, and ministry in the twenty-first century / edited by Michael Plekon, Maria Gwyn McDowell, and Elizabeth Schroeder, with a foreword by John McGuckin.

Description: Eugene, OR: Cascade Books, 2016 | Includes bibliographical references.

Identifiers: ISBN 978-1-4982-3956-1 (paperback) | ISBN 978-1-4982-3958-5 (hardcover) | ISBN 978-1-4982-3957-8 (ebook)

Subjects: LSCH: Church work | Church | Christian leadership | Christianity—21st century | Pastoral theology.

Classification: BV600.3 P73 2016 (print) | BV600.3 (ebook)

Manufactured in the U.S.A. 09/21/16

Contents

Contributors

Mary Breton is a joy-seeking, world-travelling engineer who hopes to continually grow in Christ through worship, service, and fellowship.

Nicholas Denysenko is Associate Professor of Theological Studies at Loyola-Marymount University in Los Angeles and a deacon in the Orthodox Church in America. He has published numerous books and articles in liturgical theology and the pastoral aspects of liturgy.

Adam A. J. DeVille is a professor and chair of the Department of Theology at the University of Saint Francis, Fort Wayne, Indiana. He has authored numerous articles and books on primacy, the clergy, and celibacy, and other contemporary theological issues.

John C. Frazier has served as a chaplain at Calvary Hospital hospice services in Bronx and Brooklyn New York as a certified chaplain, and has served in parish ministry at St. Gregory the Theologian Church, Wappingers Falls, New York and the Holy Virgin Protection Cathedral in New York City.

David Frost is pastor of Patterson Community Church, Patterson, New York (PCUSA). He is also lead farmer and educator at The Farm at Holmes, a sustainable CSA and educational farm project on the grounds of Holmes Presbyterian Center. His MDiv is from New York Theological Seminary in 2009.

Carol Fryer is a pastor in the Evangelical Lutheran Church in America, with decades of parish experience. More recently she is director of spiritual care at Wartburg, an historic Lutheran center for senior care in Mount Vernon, New York. Previously she served on the pastoral staff of St. Peter's Lutheran Church in Midtown Manhattan, New York City.

Kenneth J. Guest is Professor of Anthropology at Baruch College, CUNY and author of four books on cultural anthropology as well as many other articles and chapters in scholarly and popular publications. His research focuses on immigration, religion, globalization, China, and New York's Chinatown and has been featured in *The New York Times* and National Public Radio. He holds a PhD in anthropology from the City University of New York Graduate Center.

Brett Hoover is Assistant Professor of Theological Studies at Loyola-Marymount University in Los Angeles, and the author of a book and many articles on spiritual life and the parish in contemporary Catholicism. He was formerly an active priest and a member of a Catholic religious order, the Paulists.

Abbie Huff is an ordained minister in the Presbyterian Church USA, currently living in Nyack, New York. Having worked in a more traditional church setting, Abbie is currently leading a new ministry called The Nyack Project that engages people's faith and spirituality outside the walls of the church.

Wongee Joh received her MDiv degree from Drew Theological School in 2008 and serves as the pastor of a large cooperative parish consisting of six former parishes in the New York Annual Conference of the United Methodist Church. She serves on numerous local and regional ecumenical, social ministry, and Methodist boards and committees.

Justin Mathews is pastor of St. Mary of Egypt Orthodox Church in Kansas City, Missouri and director of Reconciliation Services, an outreach social ministry there. He was the former Executive Director of Focus North America, a network of Orthodox outreach ministries and has extensive experience in not-for-profit work.

Maria Gwyn McDowell is a postulant for the priesthood in the Episcopal Church and a feminist theological ethicist. Her published articles include arguments for the ordination of women to the priesthood in the Eastern Orthodox Church and the full inclusion of LGBTQ persons. She blogs at http://deiprofundis.org. She currently lives in Portland, Oregon.

John Anthony McGuckin is the Nielsen Professor of History at Union Theological Seminary, NYC, and a Professor of Byzantine Religion at Columbia University. He is an archpriest of the Orthodox Church and for over 30 years has taught in many European and American universities. He is a specialist in early medieval Christian thought and history and has published over 25 books and numerous articles on topics from NT history to Byzantine mysticism and modern theology and church history.

William C. Mills is the rector of the Nativity of the Holy Virgin Orthodox Church in Charlotte, North Carolina and the author of numerous books and articles on the scriptures and Christian spirituality.

Robert Corin Morris is the founder of Interweave, a community education outreach in Summit, New Jersey. An Episcopal priest, his ministry has centered on bringing Christian ideas into dialogue with contemporary spiritual and social concerns.

Michael Plekon is a professor in the department of Sociology/Anthropology and the Program in Religion and Culture, Baruch College of the City University of New York. He has published extensively on the search for holiness and on persons of faith in our time. He is also attached as associate priest at St. Gregory the Theologian Orthodox Church, Wappingers Falls, New York.

Sarah Hinlicky Wilson is an ordained pastor in the Evangelical Lutheran Church in America and the editor of the theological quarterly, *Lutheran Forum*. From 2008 to 2016 she served as Assistant Research Professor at the Institute for Ecumenical Research in Strasbourg, France, and continues as an adjunct of the Institute. She has published over one hundred articles on theological topics as well as the book, *Woman, Women, and the Priesthood in the Trinitarian Theology of Elisabeth Behr-Sigel.*

Foreword

—John McGuckin

FR. MICHAEL PLEKON, WHO has conceived this project, and the skillful editors Maria McDowell and Elizabeth Schroeder who have organized it to read so coherently, have put us in their debt on account of this excellent and timely new engagement with the church in our time. The idea to produce such a book, rooted in the *actualité* of Christian communities in the here-and-now, is another example of that particularity of angle that Michael Plekon brings to many of his projects, amounting to a unique eye on the world of the *ecclesia*. The word *ecclesia* is the Latinization of the Greek word for church that the New Testament uses to translate the Hebrew word for "community of God" or Qahol. Our historical journey as Christians has loaded that word, and the concept of church it describes, with so much tonnage it is difficult sometimes to think afresh. Throughout history Christian communities have had far-reaching opinions and penetrating analyses on so many things to do with contemporary society, but have often been myopic when it came to self-description and diagnosis. This book is certainly an attempt to think anew: to think real and honest. My own instinct, as an historian and a theologian by profession, is to begin with abstract nomenclature for church (ecclesiology is the discipline that we subdivided from it in the theological academy). This is perhaps a (Freudian?) way of me avoiding real down-to earth-matters, instead working from antique and generic principles. This so often happens in both academic and church circles, where we so frequently begin from the premise that we know what the church ought to be, and thus find it hard to recognize the reality because of the idea (and ideology) we have superimposed on it. That tendency as an academic abstractionist already shows in the first paragraph, which is why I for one (and I know there are many more like me) need to be taken away from my theologies and ecclesiologies and given this book as a sobering wake-up.

A strong theological tendency, especially coming from an Orthodox or Catholic perspective, is to approach the church idealistically, as the bride of Christ, the heavenly-earthly communion of the elect, the city whose gates will never be forced by the powers of evil. This "ology" of the church has deep roots and powerful authorities behind it. Such an ecclesiology derives from the words of Jesus and the teachings of the apostles and has been abstracted, from patristic times onward, to present the church as a mystical body of God's elect that cannot be reduced to merely its historical form and iteration in any given age, since it is not wholly an historical phenomenon, but rather an eschatological one. This means, for example, that the reality of the church is often described in transcendental terms (one remembers Bulgakov's impressive teachings on this score, exegeting the book of Revelation) that cannot be wholly voiced until the spirit of God completes the work of creation in the eschaton. Only then will the bride of the lamb be revealed; only then will the reality of the church be manifested and understood. Catholic tradition approached that issue of the trans-historical mystery of the church in a slightly different tone, using Paul predominantly, when it spoke of the church as the "Mystical Body of Christ." Taking its start from the diffusion of the resurrectional energy in the world, such an analysis riveted ecclesiology to a Christology of the glorified Lord, and understood his church as an expression of divine exaltation (*Anabasis*) which was mirrored in the primary function of that church on earth, to lift up glory and praise to God through Christ, in the Spirit (*Anaphora*).

These mystical ecclesiologies have produced a rich fruit, in terms of a tradition across two millennia that has been profoundly holiness-centered. The thinking about the church, its nature, and discipline in the earliest centuries of Christian existence was entirely concerned with purity matters and quality of worship in a deeply eschatological setting. Many aspects of Catholic and Orthodox thought on the church are still rooted here. And this is evidence of a strong attachment to the eschatological impetus that gave birth to the church originally. But other aspects of that tradition of exaltation formed distinct characters of church discipline in ancient times that had a long post-history as well, and may not have been so rich an apostolic exegesis. Leaders of the most ancient communities found their authority frequently contested, and on many occasions claimed that obedience to them was tantamount to obedience to Christ. But as much as absolute allegiance was claimed in the early centuries (the bishop as the stand-in for the Christ, the church as the society of the wholly pure—one thinks of the *Letters* of Ignatius of Antioch or the *Shepherd of Hermas*) so too were there many other voices in the early church that warned Christians off such possible absolutisms. It was also taught that the risen Christ never resigned his authority over his community, never gave it away to anyone else, and despite several *theologoumena* that suggested it, never removed his attention from his lordly governance of his community. Similarly the canons of the developing synods made strong counter-statements to the effect that even bishops had to be subject to communal wisdom in Christian affairs; no one under Christ had absolute authority in the church on earth; and the church itself had to be recognized as the community of a purity of the Lord's, not of their own making, and thus a society comprised of sinners whose blessedness could not be relied on, except as rising always from repentance and reconciliation. That was the fundament of the resurrectional energy Christ had bestowed on the world—reconciliation (*katallage*), which the church had a fundamental duty to represent to that world in so much need of reconciliation then, as indeed now. The Catholic and Orthodox ecclesiologies (that is "doctrines of church") were beautifully transcendental, mystical in character and uplifting. They have also tended to make their adherents look to ideals more than realities, even when realities seemed to contradict their exalted analyses. It is a fine thing to walk down the street looking only at the stars. The risk of course is to fall over the fire hydrant.

In the Protestant Reformation, much changed in regard to that earlier structure of ecclesiology. Much resistance against late medieval forms of authority structure joined with resistance to many aspects of earlier Christian doctrines, and produced a new ferment of thinking. Many older structures fell before the reformers' desire to institute new polities and teachings. The very self-definition of the church was thought out anew. But paradoxically, some of the oldest reflections on the nature of the church were given a new stress by the elevation of the New Testament as the highest of all authorities in the Christian commune. The notion of the church as the pure body was thus re-emphasized, absolutized in a sense, and the long centuries where the synodical canonical tradition of dealing with the realpolitik of a sinful community needing pastoral care and accommodation was set aside wholesale. Mystical ideas that had had a long continuance into medieval times were also swept aside in several new iterations that saw the church as a kind of synonym for the collective of a community of prayer. Such a discipline had a large following in the radical reform movement and accounted even for new church communities that took ecclesiology into the variegated and disparate world of denominationalism. From the nineteenth century onward, as the Protestant reliance on the concept of sacred canon as a fundamental guide began to dwindle in the light of the impact of historical biblical criticism, its approach to church became more and more non-transcendental, more and more rooted as a notion of a local assembly gathered together for prayer and action. Of course the biblical ideas also continued, but with a weakening sense of historical rootedness (what did Calvin have to do with Presbyterianism in the late twentieth century?) and biblical authority (what was left of the sacredness of Scripture, when late twentieth-century biblical critics in the Protestant schools had so largely tried to relativize it?) there could be no doubt that the Protestant sense of church had been profoundly conflicted.

In the middle of the twentieth century the Latin American missions, which were proving to be a new conflict area between the two great Western communions, generated a new ecclesiology for both Catholics and Protestants that was seized upon and developed from the concept of base-communities (*communités du bas*) into widely adopted forms of liberation theology, which prioritized the sense of the church as a society of prayer and worship dedicated to the application of justice. In many ways this was so widely adopted by the wider communions that it began to form a commonality among Catholics and Protestants on matters of church identity that had not been in operation for the previous five hundred years; and it brought, together with its insistence that the work of the church was social justice, a renewed sense of social realism. Such a movement had a span of operation from the time of *Gaudium et Spes* at the Second Vatican Council (known in English as "The Church in the Modern World") into the twenty-first century. It was a dynamic time of renewal that laid positive stress on ecumenical cooperation. There was, concomitant with it, even a sense that deep-seated, entrenched differences between churches could be overcome in a new wave of cooperation, mutual respect, and renewal.

But by the end of the twentieth century, a period marked by innumerable wars of increasing savagery, the fabric of the churches showed no great renewal, and their impact on the social fabric proved hard to secure. European church life entered a bleak decline. Church buildings in multiple architectural forms, from gothic to classical, were turned into restaurants, gyms, and carpet showrooms, as their congregations died off. Buildings became echoing and empty spaces for the tiny number of congregants who could no longer financially sustain the buildings' maintenance. Crises began to hit the seminaries and theology schools, and the supply of ministers ran dry in many places where it had been thought they would never need to alter entrenched ways of thinking and behaving. Such things had been setting in, like mold, for generations before, but it was only when the financial aspects began to bite hard that churches were forced to look them in the face. Here was the place where the transcendental concept of the church of God met the reality of a local community meeting in a brick or stone edifice, which they also called the church by extension, and often which they could not differentiate from their theological idea. In Greek it was different. The "church of God" the scripture spoke about as a concept was *ekklesia*, and the church building was *naos*, temple or shrine. The Latin and Saxon had tied the two ideas together semantically in what was, at least for a period of social decline, a very unhelpful way.

And this is why this present book is so valuable, for it approaches ecclesiology from the real world of experienced and reflective peoples' accounts of ministerial life in a variety of church settings. All the writers are able, with grace and effectiveness, to write as men and women of deep and engaged experience, but also with profound religious, that is theological and ecclesiological, sensibility. The authors demonstrate at times an almost painfully honest expression of what their ecclesial experience was really like. Many of them are clearly the kind of pastor that one would wish was near if one was ever in trouble requiring a sensitive and intelligent counselor. Among these, the book's conceiving imaginer is pre-eminent. Fr. Plekon himself has deep pastoral skills honed over many decades exercising a priestly ministry in the Orthodox New World. He is also a skilled theologian with a wide-ranging awareness of theological matters and spiritual traditions as his previous books, outstanding in their field, will readily testify. But all these gifts come together in a new and exciting way in this present volume of collected studies he brought together. For he is also a skilled professional social philosopher, and has taught the subject at university level for many years past. In this volume his many different skill sets come together in an electrifying way.

His idea behind the volume was to ask the question: what happens when the idea of church as a fixed community of believers, gathered round a set ritual, in a specific bricked and mortared place (the idea of church that has carried most Americans forward as a default idea for generations past) starts to falter under the pressures of late modernity, and communities dwindle to the point where the actual church building is now no longer the haven and castle of the community, but its financial bane, and when the youngest person in the gathering is in their sixties? The diverse array of essays makes for a gripping read throughout. They are all confessional to a large extent, and they seize one's attention because of the unflinching honesty with which they communicate to the reader.

There is no doubt in my mind that this book ought to be on the compulsory reading list for all seminarians. It would be the basis for a superb seminar text for a group of intelligent people preparing for ministry, to go through each chapter as a case study. Too often young people (though many offering themselves for ministry today are second or third careerists) leave with the qualifying MDiv only to find the outside world of leading (often obstinate and obtuse) church communities is hardly what they expected. Many times these communities are remote from what they felt they were dedicating their energies to on the basis of a former positive experience in the worship community that they came out of in order to go to seminary. The essays here allow us to draw on the experiences of a large array of ministers telling us the warts and whole pictures of their day-to-day engagements with the administration of local churches. The essays cover congregational burn-out, as well as pastoral burn-out, but also offer hope and encouragement that the richest resources in the church are always going to be people filled with love; and that with Christ's abiding presence, refreshed by prayer and sacrament, the church will always remain alive—just not always where you expect it will be.

When now-aging ravers formerly heard the announcement in packed auditoria, "Elvis has left the building," it was time for everyone to give up and go home. If the church has "left the building," what, one wonders, should be our response? With the mounting evidence of so much decline in church attendance and infrastructure, one has an immediate sense of anxiety, and perhaps fear of loss. But is it a bad thing that so many communities of Christians are losing the buildings their grandparents once strove to build with pennies they could ill afford, but contributed to with passion and pride in their hearts to establish a sign of the kingdom of God among them? How many communities are tied to old loyalties of stones and bricks, and cannot bear to face the weekly realities of dwindling numbers and enfeebled aspirations among groups of worshippers where the average age is phenomenally high; and where little energy remains for building a lively sense of community; and the spiritual temperature of the group may be moderate to low, certainly not helped by a tired liturgical and spiritual life in common? Young people coming into such places, such families of worship, find little to keep them there, little to draw them there if they did not have a family connection in the first place. What can be done if the church is not just leaving the building, but leaking out from the building? Is it a cause for distress? Maybe so if one has never thought about it.

But if this book brings bad news for the first time, at least it is consoling in alerting us to the evident fact that we have been living in ostrich-like anxiety, with our heads in the sand. But the alarm, once duly registered, is not one that should cause terminal despair, argue many of the writers in this book. It is certainly a cause for focused attention, as they lay clear before us. And attentiveness among the leaders of ministry today will surely set the tone for this generation and the next of what fabric and condition the churches will have in the century ahead. One third of the present generation of young people in the United States describe themselves as having no religion at all. If it does nothing else than give us a clear rinse of cold reality, this book will have served its purpose. For those who wish to think beyond that wake-up call, it can also offer rich wisdom for broaching the need for nothing less than a new and renovative mission to re-establish the church in our time.

Acknowledgments

MUCH GRATITUDE is due here.

To all those who were willing to contribute their reflections on faith, the parish and ministry in the twenty-first century. Your thoughts, hopes, regrets and more will now be shared by many.

Thanks also to John McGuckin for immersing himself in these reflections and then introducing them.

I am especially grateful to Maria McDowell and Elizabeth Schroeder, the co-editors, for their dedication and amazing work in bringing the text into a publishable condition. And thanks to all those at Cascade who welcomed this project and helped it move forward.

Lastly, I am sure all of us who participated have teachers, students, family and friends and fellow members of the people of God to thank, throughout the years of our living and working in the church.

We know, and this volume attests to Irenaeus of Lyons' words: Ubi enim ecclesia, ibi et spiritus dei; et ubi spiritus dei, illic ecclesia et omnis gratia, spiritus autem veritas—"Where the church is, there is also the Spirit of God and where the Spirit of God is, there is also the church and all grace. The Spirit is truth" (*Adv. Hares.* III, 24, 1).

—*Michael Plekon*

1

Belonging to the Christian Community in
the Twenty-first Century, When "the Church
Has Left the Building"

—Michael Plekon

Is everything in the Church changeless and in what sense is the
Church herself changeless? Such are the questions that, under
various aspects, stir modern Christian thought; . . . what should
and must be the attitude of the Church towards modern life and
its problems. If everything in the Church is changeless . . . then this
means that modern life concerns the Church only to the degree
in which the Church must keep and preserve her sanctity in the
life of the world in order to bring it to the time of fulfillment. This
presupposes that the Church . . . is withdrawn from the world, that
there is one road—from the world into the Church—but there is
no road from the Church into the world. This would be correct
only if the Church, together with its members, could leave the
world. But she does not lead them out of the world ("since then
you would need to go out of the world" [1 Cor 5:10]) and, accord-
ingly, the Church cannot leave her members in the world alone.
The Church faces the world, not the desert. She abides in the world
and builds in the world until "the fullness of time."[1]

From individual paths to communities of faith

THESE AFFIRMATIVE WORDS ON the church in the world are not new. They
come from a collection of essays published almost eighty years ago in Paris
by a progressive group of writers concerned with the gospel in the twentieth

---

1. Afanasiev, "The Church's Canons," 31–32.

century, with the church in the modern world of revolutions, wars, and economic crises. These lines come from one of the finest scholars on the history of the church—Nicholas Afanasiev, an émigré Russian Orthodox priest and theologian who taught at St. Sergius Institute in Paris from the 1930s till his death in 1966. Afanasiev was a polymath, capable across several fields. He was a specialist in the history of the church councils, canon law, the New Testament, liturgical and church history, both ancient and modern.

As much as Afanasiev concerned himself with the patterns of church life in the first few centuries, he was intensely aware of the changes that occur in the world around the church, as well as the changes that take place in the church itself. The passage quoted above is a discerning statement on the relationship, indeed, the mission of the church to the world. If the church is here "for the life of the world," to proclaim the good news of the kingdom, then the church must also be "of the world," connected to it, located within it, interacting with it. At least, so the parables of the New Testament suggest, in the perspective of scholar Amy-Jill Levine.[2]

I first saw the expression "The church has left the building" in a post on the *Religious News Service* (RNS). As Brett Hoover notes in his reflection, the origin of the phrase lies with Elvis. In order to clear halls of his riotous fans after concerts, there would be an announcement: "Elvis has left the building." Here the expression highlights intense change within the church. Not only does the church change for its own existence, it also does so for the life of the world. And the church cannot avoid the many changes that have come and will continue to come from other transformations in our society, demographic changes long in process.

This book is a collection of narratives about all of this. What you have before you is a gathering of first-hand reflections—stories really—from a diverse group of Christians, lay as well as ordained. While each has a distinctive experience of the church in our time, all of them—I should say all of us—have something to say about the many changes in our society and how these are affecting our faith, the parish, and pastoral work. First, though, I should say a little about how this collection came to be.

2. Levine, *Short Stories by Jesus*.

Changes and the Churches

Robert Putnam and David Campbell recently published a probing examination of religion in American society and life.[3] Putnam earlier looked at the decline of community and more recently has explored how we treat our children.[4] Their study of American religion was based on existing research and on a rigorous two-panel survey of over 3,000 respondents (almost 2,000 in the second wave), entitled "Faith Matters." In many ways their findings echo the important work of Robert Bellah and his associates decades ago in *Habits of the Heart* and *The Good Society,* as well as the work of Robert Wuthnow, Mark Chaves, and James Davison Hunter, among others. Putnam and Campbell offer an optimistic assessment of religion in America despite significant historical and generational changes in religiosity and the division between liberals and conservatives.

Despite claims that America, in its increasing diversity, is becoming less actively religious, Putnam and Campbell argue that religion remains dynamic and influential. For that matter, scrutiny of America's religious past yields images of a far from pious people, as Finke and Stark argue.[5] Putnam and Campbell conclude that after a decline in religiosity in the 1960s and the swing to the religious right in the 1980s, the gap between secular liberals and religious conservatives has deepened. The clashes of the older "culture wars" and challenges that the churches face from social change continue. The legalization of same sex marriages; the larger question of the civil rights of LGBT people; the place of women in society; the size and role of government; the growing economic inequality in America; and, more recently, the specter of racism—these are but a few of the issues confronting the churches. In some surveys, the sluggishness of churches to change, to become more accepting and tolerant, seems to have driven younger people away.

Yet Putnam and Campbell also see growth in interfaith marriages and in personal ties among persons of different faith communities—a new and very different set of ways in which religion is bringing people together and perhaps making some more open and tolerant. They find religion still important in American life, although with some significant changes. These changes, in sum, point to an aging church population as well as a declining

a decline in religiosity (twice living and worship)

3. Putnam and Campbell, *American Grace.*

4. Putnam, *Bowling Alone; Our Kids.*

5. Finke and Starke, *The Churching of America 1776–1990.*

3

one. Those religious "nones," claiming no membership or activity in communities of faith, have increased in number and, as the most recent Pew survey indicates, a drop of over 7 percent of the population who identify as Christian occurred between 2007 to 2015.[6] Mark Chaves, a longtime student of American religious activity, sees consistent, overall decline.[7] A recent Public Religion Research Institute study found that Americans significantly overestimate the frequency of their church attendance, what

6. Pew Research Center, "America's Changing Religious Landscape."

7. A further but very brief look at some research about religion in America is important here. The American Congregations Study (2008) put out by the Hartford Institute for Religious Research (HIRR) points to decline: worship attendance, poor financial health, and weak spiritual life. Parishes are aging: individuals aged sixty-five or older make up one quarter to one half of the membership of six out of ten parishes. The 2008 Pew US Religious Landscape Survey, with a sample of 35,000, had quite similar findings. 28 percent have left their religion of origin for another or none at all. 44 percent have switched denominations. 16 percent are unaffiliated (atheist, agnostic, unaffiliated)—this and other studies note that the number of religious "nones" is steadily rising. If immigrant numbers are controlled, Catholics have suffered the biggest losses. More recent Pew data, October 2012, indicate almost 20 percent are "nones." (http://www.pewforum.org/unaffiliated/nones-on-the-rise.aspx).

More positively, 70 percent say they are open and non-absolutist about their faith, and that they believe there are other paths. More than 50 percent say religion is important in their lives, and attend services and pray frequently.

The HIRR Decade of Change 2000–2010 study, directed by David Roozen, notes that by 2010, one in four congregations had fifty or fewer attendees in their pews. The study observed that megachurches that had doubled in size were beginning to shrink. This same study found significant aging among congregation members. 53 percent of members of oldline churches were 65 or older, only 10 percent were between 18–34, and in another decade 50 percent of these churches will lose one third of their members. Financial health of congregations was also found to be declining, especially after the 2008 great recession. More positively, there was growth in the number of immigrants in congregations, and growth in use of electronic media, in use of different worship styles and in connections with other faiths. In his studies, Mark Chaves used data from NORC General Social Survey (GSS). He found that there is stability but no real increase across all measures of religiosity. On closer inspection and with further assessment for Chaves, this means that for the first time in the history of study of religious behavior in America, there is generally decline. It is not possible to find indicators of increase. This is so despite other findings, namely that 64 percent say they know God exists, 69 percent pray frequently, and 25 percent attend services weekly. Worship attendance dramatically decreased from the '50s through the '90s and has continued decreasing. There was also a small but steady decrease in belief in God, from 99 percent in the '50s to 92 percent in 2008. Chaves' *American Congregations at the Beginning of the 21st Century*/ NCS study echoes findings from the above studies. Finally, the 2012 Gallup Poll found that only 44 percent of Americans were confident in and trusted in religious institutions. https://scholars.duke.edu/display/pub966886.

some have calling "fibbing" about the practice of their faith.[8] Immigration patterns have and will continue to have enormous impact on who Americans are, ethnically speaking.[9] The 2014 General Social Survey confirmed earlier findings. 34 percent now report never attending church except for events like weddings and funerals.[10]

These are very broad, sweeping findings about religion and life in America, and in many ways, they are startling and troubling. Maybe they are surprising to those who seldom find themselves inside a church building, but in numerous conversations over the past few years, I have found that SBNR these realities are well known to members of the church, pastors and laity alike. Nancy Ammerman argues that the so-called SBNR divide, "spiritual but not religious," is not an accurate description of how Americans really are.[11] Brett Hoover has thought carefully about the impact of demographic and cultural changes on Catholic parishes.[12] Research by Diana Butler Bass describes the characteristics of vital congregations, ones that have revived or stayed alive.[13] Such parishes make worship central. They also have a strong sense of community, as well as the desire for learning together and outreach to the surrounding neighborhood. It is important not to get it wrong—there are parishes that are declining, in many cases because of demographic and other changes over which they have no control. But there are also parishes that are intentional and vital, and while these are diverse, Bass found them to consistently have the aforementioned qualities.

In looking at persons of faith in other research and writing I have done, as well as in my own experience, it was clear that they relied on communities of faith.[14] They were members of communities, not just traditions of thought, but concrete parishes, church bodies, and in a few cases religious orders. To speak of communities of faith immediately sets us into the turbulence, the controversy of change. Even those churches which pride themselves on being traditional, of changing little or not at all, are experiencing change. In the past several decades there has been a great deal of talk about church life amid change—growth, renewal, re-rooting, and reform. Not

8. PRRI, "I Know What You Did Last Sunday."

9. Passel and Cohn, "US Population Projections 2005–2050."

10. NORC, "General Social Survey."

11. Ammerman, *Sacred Stories, Spiritual Tribes.*

12. Hoover, "Generation and Culture: Future Parish Life in the United States," 218–22.

13. Bass, *Christianity for the Rest of Us.*

14. Plekon, *Living Icon, Hidden Holiness.*

long ago there was fascination with megachurches such as Willow Creek. Founder of Willow Creek, Bill Hybels, has reconsidered his project with a healthy dose of self-criticism earlier absent from megachurch evangelizing.

The "emergent/emerging church" movement in the past decade or so has been raising questions about what church is in the twenty-first century. Is it keeping the roof on this historical but now impractical building? Is it re-rooting venerable parishes in neighborhoods completely different in population and use than when they were begun? Is it facing the reality that the "village has vanished," as Diana Butler Bass puts it, that most of our formerly "village parishes" no longer exist? Many parishioners no longer live in the immediate neighborhood where the church bell can be heard, where people can walk to and from the sanctuary. The homogenous ethnic communities which established and built the cathedral-like church buildings found in many locations no longer exist. It is becoming rare to find multi-generational families in parishes—children and grandchildren relocate for education and employment. Increasingly, intermarriage or marriage outside of the ethnic/church of origin is the norm. Carol Howard Merritt has been an important voice describing and responding to many of these changes.[15] She has addressed the very reality addressed here, of the church "leaving the building."[16] Change, even for the most conservative and traditional of Christian churches, is now a constant reality.

Churches and buildings

Down through the centuries the church has inhabited all kinds of buildings, beginning with the homes of people like Andronicus and Junia, Aquila and Priscilla, and Lydia. Paul preached outdoors in the *agora*, where Jews met to pray on the beach or in rented rooms. Eventually both private homes and public buildings were repurposed for the assembly of the faithful. One such house was excavated some years ago in Dura-Europos in Syria. Roman gathering halls and basilicas became Christian places of worship. Eventually, emperors like Justinian would call on architects to create new spaces larger than any previously known in the ancient world. I refer to the great church of the "new Rome," Constantinople, Hagia Sophia. Other

15. Merritt, *Tribal Church.* Also see her blog, "Tribal Church," at www.christiancentury.org/blogs/tribal-church.

16. Merritt, "Keeping the Church Weird." http://www.christiancentury.org/article/2014–04/keeping-church-weird.

great churches would emerge in Ravenna, Monreale, Rome, Venice, Kyiv, Chartres, Canterbury, Paris, and London, across the empire, across nations that were officially Christian. The history of making churches would continue on to our own time with Corbusier, Breuer, and Saarinen. More recently, church has returned to much smaller, more intimate house-church settings, such as St. Lydia's Dinner Church, founded by Pastor Emily Scott in Brooklyn NY.[17]

Yet despite this "edifice complex," the great cathedral and the humble country church both are but houses of the people of God, spaces for God and worship. Despite all the changes that will be addressed here, it is not the case that the church is through, bypassed, over. The presence of the Spirit in the body of Christ—this will remain always. However, the structure—the institution that houses it—is another matter.

One hears that "the church has left the building" in many ways. I began to hear about this indirectly, from afar really, as the parish to which I am attached has been remarkably stable and sustainable for decades now.

Over the past few years, as mentioned, conversations with fellow clergy from various churches and with the seminarian interns from our parish started to coalesce. I visited a former intern at his parish in the coal region of Northeastern Pennsylvania, where my father's family lived and my uncle served as priest for over fifty years. It was a powerful experience. The decline of so many parishes in that area, of all denominations, is connected with other accounts I had heard from urban as well as rural locations. It was not that people were abandoning the church, rejecting Christian faith, liturgy, or life. Rather, there had been profound changes in the demographics. With mines and factories gone, the second and third generations of immigrants moved away to find jobs. Very beautiful, cathedral-like churches were now attended by a few dozen retirees. The challenge of keeping buildings heated and cooled, of maintaining the roof and other structural aspects as well as supporting a pastor and family—this was becoming impossible. In some churches, as noted, the problems were addressed by forming multi-point parishes. This might consist of combinations of formerly independent units now linked together served by one rotating pastor, or combining more than one parish in different sanctuaries on various Sundays.

A colleague, who is now a diocesan administrator in the Episcopal Church, described a growing number of small town and rural parishes

---

17. See St. Lydia's, http://www.stlydias.org/. Scott, "We've Seen Megachurch. But How About Micro-Church?"

*'No building No Church'

which wanted their own pastor. While in theory there were available clergy, in practice there were further complications. One was that of matching these parishes with "worker priests," that is, clergy with full-time occupations unable to relocate from their homes or jobs to fill the parish spots. More serious is the reality of parishes that simply cannot support a pastor and have difficulty keeping the building open, heated, the bills paid. Across the range of churches in America, whether rural or urban, this is a reality.

A friend in her late sixties told me that she is now the youngest member of what was once a suburban mission parish plant—a community now mostly in their eighties—with a "good Sunday" meaning perhaps thirty at the liturgy. All across New York State where I live, Methodist, Presbyterian, Episcopal, and Lutheran parishes are gathered into clusters, with one pastor caring for two, three, four, or more on a rotating basis. Even in the bucolic, affluent Hudson Valley where I live, many parishes are cared for by "weekend pastors," as well as retired and "worker priests" with full time professions, who live and work elsewhere, traveling up for Sunday services. The use of lay or local pastors by some church bodies is another strategy, though not without problems.[18] Such a pastor is someone in the course of their theological education or specially trained for ministry in their home parish, either with another occupation or retired. Most of these parishes have until now been kept open, somehow. But it is no longer an oddity to drive past a church that has become a restaurant or antiques dealer or even a private home. There will be personal reflections here by pastors, one Methodist, the other Presbyterian, who are serving two of these historical parishes now struggling to survive in the twenty-first century. There will be another by a priest trying to renew and re-root a once ethnic inner city parish.

All of us have faced some of the issues mentioned. Some of the most significant challenges come from demographic changes—the "village vanishing," the former economic bases for parishes disappearing, their members relocating elsewhere for employment and education. All of these were to be seen in the Pennsylvania parish of our intern but in time I realized very similar patterns were showing themselves in many other places. Another colleague and former intern reported massive out-movement during the recession from Charlotte, North Carolina. I saw this even very close to home, in the Lutheran parish in which I had served almost thirty years ago, in the Eastern Orthodox parish to which I was attached, and also the

18. Wood, "Called But Not Ordained," and Wheeler, "The Problems with Lay Pastors."

parish within walking distance of my home, a tiny, historic, rural Methodist congregation.

The decline of manufacturing and mining in the Northeast and the disappearance of the steel industry and of heavy manufacturing in the Midwest have directly affected church membership, with a consistent decades-long pattern of out-migration in search of employment. And to these must be added the diversity of church backgrounds which is characteristic of American society. Increased intermarriage changes the once-homogenous background of parish members. Sometimes marrying outside one's denomination does not affect membership, but very often it does change identity and affiliation. When the economic base for a parish disappears, as well as generations of members, the consequences are dwindling congregations. Left behind are parishes barely able to remain open. With parishes unable to support a pastor, unable to meet their other operating expenses, the reality of this change is already with us, and the number of such congregations is growing.

A quick assessment might be that there is a clergy shortage—looking at the situation with Roman Catholic parishes and some other church bodies could lead one to this conclusion. However, in most cases it is precisely the opposite—not a shortage of clergy but a *shortage of viable parishes that could support a pastor.* This is so, in some cases, because of redundant congregations—parishes that formerly were ethnic in origin but of the same church body or parishes of multiple church bodies, now in communion with each other. The presence of several Greek and Russian Orthodox churches and even more Roman Catholic parishes in a small coal town in Pennsylvania would be an example, or the same in a formerly urban industrial area in New Jersey. Likewise in Brooklyn, parishes of formerly autonomous Lutheran church bodies, now long merged into the ELCA, would be another, as would be multiple plants of parishes of the same denomination, whether Presbyterian, Episcopal, or Methodist. Where I live in the Hudson valley, many formerly independent small towns all have their very own set of denominational outposts, whether Lutheran, Methodist, or Episcopalian—now within minutes' drive of each other, clearly duplications. Yet efforts to regroup and re-root these bodies into a regional parish have been resisted. Catholic parishes have constructed new very large exurban plants, when members have long lived far from the older inner city buildings. Seating hundreds of people, these new buildings enable a single priest with many lay eucharistic ministers to service very large congregations for the Sunday masses. Perhaps the Catholics could qualify for clergy shortage, but they too have many parishes, both urban and rural, that are no longer viable. Cardinal Dolan of the archdiocese of New York, Cardinal O'Malley of Boston, and Bishop Robert Rimbo in the Lutheran Metropolitan Synod of New York have all called for parish renewal and amalgamation, along with parish closings.

In addition to the demographic factors noted, it might be tempting to think that the decline of parishes is also due to religious indifference on the part of individuals—persons not brought up in the faith or others who have come to reject religious belonging. However, further surveys of Americans do not consistently support this. *American Grace* did not find much drift, but Pew studies are documenting a significant turning away from religious identification or belief, not just decrease in denominational and congregational membership. The survey data cited earlier is stark with the ever rising of "nones," the aging nature of congregations, and a signifi-cant distancing of millenials from all sorts of institutional belonging and identification, religion included.[19] However, after a great deal of discussion and research, I myself have come to see that perhaps there is a place once more for smaller, simpler parishes, ones in which the pastor works in a profession or job like other members, with congregations where genuine communal commitment and engagement exists, and less of the "Christ-mas/Easter" and "rites of passage" syndromes of rare appearances is found.

Personal reflections on faith, parish life, and ministry in the twenty-first century

What follows is something like a memoir or autobiographical narrative, or in simplest terms, the stories of people of faith. Nancy Ammerman, in her fascinating studies of religious communities, has very effectively used the stories of both individuals and congregations.[20] Likewise, Tanya Luhrmann has listened to believers' accounts of their direct experience of God in her startling book.[21] So much of religious literature is of this personal, narrative sort. It is presented here for its power and beauty.

19. Pew Research Center, "Millenials in Adulthood." Also, Pew Research Center, "America's Changing Religious Landscape."

20. Ammerman, *Sacred Stories, Spiritual Tribes* and *Congregation & Community.*

21 Luhrmann, *When God Talks Back.*

Some of the first person accounts you will read here started as conversations, phone calls, and email exchanges among myself and colleagues or friends. As you will see, the reflections are as diverse as the women and men who wrote them. Originally, these were exchanges about how we live or practice parish life—worship, fellowship, study, outreach—when so much about who were are, and where we live and work has changed.

Some of the conversations communicate frustration and worry. Some tell of deep disappointment. There are some that are full of pain and sadness and in at least one case church life became so awful that the reflection really could not be completed and contributed. It is not the case that all these very honest, moving stories have a happy ending. One writer kept postponing the sending of a contribution because things in life and work kept changing—rapidly, profoundly. Which story was to be told?

Some of the writers dig down into childhood, into the experience of faith nurtured by family, language, music, and the comforting, soft quilt—if I can call it that—of faith and tradition. As with Rachel Held Evans' recent narrative, there are in these reflections conflict and hurt where one might expect people of faith to be nurturing joy and a sense of acceptance.[22] Only those who have lived in a community of faith know that for all the peace and joy, there is also friction, anger, even destructive behavior.

Yet, I think you will find—as I did—hope here, as well as gratitude and determination. While I do not know each of the writers equally well, I can say that all really share themselves here as few authors in spiritual literature do. I must warn readers that this is not a "how-to" book, not a guide to renewing or sustaining or protecting faith and parish life today, or for increasing pastoral effectiveness. There is substantial literature along those lines, but that is not the aim here.

I have become convinced that Diana Butler Bass's path is the one that needs more study and reflection.[23] I mean by this the cluster of questions she asks which are so threatening to church leaders and seminary faculty, and sadly often invisible to many parish pastors and churchgoers. Namely, what are the shape, the arrangements, and the activities—in short, the life—of a Christian community, a local church, or parish in the twenty-first century? The voices you will hear in this collection will have a great deal to say on these matters.

22. Evans, *Searching for Sunday*.
23. Bass, *Christianity for the Rest of Us*.

This is a complex reality, for it includes not only the worship life of the parish but how it organizes itself as a community, how it prays and experiences grace and faith outside the services, in ordinary, daily tasks. It also involves where the church locates itself. Some buildings will not be financially sustainable. It must also include how the community will raise funds, what it will do with its financial resources, and what kind of outreach it has to the local neighborhood and other parts of the church and the world. Equally related is the relationship of the parish to other churches in the same area, without regard for their tradition. The extent to which a community continues to learn, to challenge itself and be challenged, to be able to see change not as a threat are the characteristics that Butler Bass found to be indicative of intentional and dynamic parishes. As you will read, these are also the characteristics of those who have contributed their personal experiences in the essays to follow.

To confront the fascinating, perplexing, even disturbing changes for faith, for parish life, and for ministry of the twenty-first century, is the task of the essays gathered here. This is not a survey such as the one Diana Butler Bass conducted. Rather, gathered here are personal reflections on living and working in the local church of the parish in the twenty-first century and in everyday life, family, work, and neighborhood, by a number of lay people and pastors. The personal accounts of pastoral ministry and parish life by, among others, Lillian Daniel, Martin Copenhaver, Barbara Brown Taylor, and Richard Lischer are examples of this kind of reflection that have received critical praise.[24] What such an approach cannot yield in breadth it nevertheless does provide in depth and detail.

Here, in these gathered accounts, you will not find recipes, that is, models or programs for bigger, more financially secure Christian communities. Online and at conferences such plans are offered. There are numerous individual efforts at proposing more effective models.[25] Mainstream denominations seem to need to have new versions of these every few years. The first person accounts here might offer glimpses of how—despite decreasing numbers, aging congregations, and dwindling resources—the life of the people of God in a particular location survives, even thrives.

It is far beyond the purpose of this essay and this volume to seriously take a stab at the many complicated questions that confront us—what the

---

24. Daniel and Copenhaver, *This Odd and Wondrous Calling*; Taylor, *Leaving Church* and *An Altar in the World*; Lischer, *Open Secrets*; Walford, *The Spirit's Tether*.

25. See, for example, Jones, *Facing Decline, Finding Hope*.

church is and does—much less address the long term impacts of all the changes taking place in the world in which the church finds itself today. Our world is changing and that means as we come closer to our own micro-worlds, our neighborhoods, towns, families, and households are also changing. Of course, how could it be otherwise—our parishes, the local churches are changing too, and profoundly.

But this has always been the case. We get trapped and fooled into thinking things were better in the recent past, in the proverbial good old days. We are creatures of habit, shaped by familiarity and custom. We are then surprised at how different we look in photos from a decade or two or three ago! Often we delude ourselves into thinking that at least at church, nothing changes.

But, Jesus's first words in Matthew's Gospel are that we must change, turn inside out, be transformed; for the kingdom of heaven is very near, right in our midst. To see it this way is to understand the church as part of a larger living tradition. The essays to follow here are narratives of this living tradition. They include both the religious past and journeys of the writers, as well as a number of experiences close to the present—some positive and encouraging, others more negative, less hopeful. Our first person accounts will surely raise more questions than they answer.

One reflection, by a specialist in liturgy, describes how worship can draw people together, even if economically and culturally challenged as immigrants. The lessons he learned from growing up in a Ukrainian community in the Midwest resonate today with the smaller, struggling parishes in both urban and rural locations. Another contributor describes the arc that took her and her family from a very tribal ethnic church community out into mainstream America, and then into tiny, embattled parishes founded in the eighteenth century. Another ordained clergy person will narrate the journey from suburban New Jersey and the taken-for-granted comfort of the parish in which he was raised to the challenge of North Carolina, where everyone is from somewhere else. Yet another pastor-author sketches the journey of his seminary hopes and expectations through the often adversarial realities of the institutional church and its politics. In the end, he found his place in outreach ministry to the urban homeless, hungry, and poor. A semi-retired Episcopal priest looks back on over forty years of ministry and parish life and shares what that long journey taught him and where it led him. Another pastor who has experience in both small town and urban parishes, and now in chaplaincy, shares her journey. A young pastor learned how to find a place when there are no parish placements. There are also some other very powerful personal accounts, of how younger pastors have experienced changes in faith and in vocation in their own lives. One pastor agreed to care for a struggling, inner city ethnic parish during her graduate studies only to find it had become a dues-paying club, concerned only with financial survival. This was a profoundly disturbing experience in her first parish. Several other pastors share their struggles in failing parishes and the politics of church life.

But it is not only clergy who offer reflections. Lay people too share their experiences, some hopeful, others bittersweet, some painful. The perspectives of women on the parish, faith, and pastoral work and how these connect with personal life are crucial to this collection. Then again, personal experience weighs in heavily. One contributor looks at how necessary community is, far more so than a building—this from several memorable stints in communal living. Another shares grief over finding herself, at least temporarily, to be homeless from a churchly perspective. A head chaplain at a church-based community for the elderly thinks back on earlier pastoral postings. She is grateful for an as-yet-unbroken series of welcomes and roots in ecclesial communities she has experienced. Still another, a professor, reflects on the movement within his tradition as he himself departs active ministry.

Given the diversity of contributors—Episcopal, Methodist, Lutheran, Catholic, Eastern Orthodox, and more, lay women and men and ordained—there are very different assessments with widely varying backgrounds. The spiritual journeys are intriguing. The frustrations experienced by the writers in faith, parish life, and pastoral ministry are very challenging. Yet, what is most encouraging, and a thread that unifies such diverse narratives, is the confidence that the church as the people of God will continue and be a place of community, communion, and service. From Peter Berger to Charles Taylor to José Casanova and many other students of religion in our time, the former consensus about progressive secularization has been rejected.[26] The church may be "leaving the building," but it is still "in the house."

Bibliography

Afanasiev, Nicholas. "The Church's Canons: Changeable or Unchangeable." In *Tradition Alive*, edited by Michael Plekon, 31–46. Lanham, MD: Rowan & Littlefield, 2003.

26. Taylor, *A Secular Age*; Casanova, "Rethinking Secularization."

Ammerman, Nancy Tatom. *Congregation & Community*. New Brunswick, NJ: Rutgers University Press, 2001.

———. *Sacred Stories, Spiritual Tribes*. Oxford: Oxford University Press, 2014.

Bass, Diana Butler. *Christianity for the Rest of Us*. New York: HarperOne, 2006.

Casanova, José. "Rethinking Secularization: A Global Comparative Perspective." *The Hedgehog Review* 8.1–2 (2006) 7–22.

Chaves, M., S. Anderson, and J. Byassee. "American Congregations at the Beginning of the 21st Century: A Report from the National Congregations Study." https://scholars.duke.edu/display/pub966886. Duke University, 2008.

Daniel, Lillian, and Martin Copenhaver. *This Odd and Wondrous Calling*. Grand Rapids: Eerdmans, 2009.

Evans, Rachel Held. *Searching for Sunday*. Nashville, TN: Thomas Nelson, 2015.

Finke, Roger, and Rodney Starke. *The Churching of America 1776–1990*. New Brunswick, NJ: Rutgers University Press, 1992.

Hoover, Brett C. "Generation and Culture: Future Parish Life in the United States." *Origins* 41:14 (2011) 218–22.

Jones, Jeffrey D. *Facing Decline, Finding Hope: New Possibilities for Faithful Churches*. Lanham, MD: Rowan & Littlefield, 2015.

Levine, Amy Jill. *Short Stories by Jesus*. New York: HarperOne, 2014.

Lischer, Richard. *Open Secrets*. New York: Doubleday, 2001.

Luhrmann, T. M. *When God Talks Back*. New York: Knopf, 2012.

Merritt, Carol Howard. "Keeping the Church Weird." *The Christian Century* 131.9 (2014). http://www.christiancentury.org/article/2014–04/keeping-church-weird.

———. *Reframing Hope: Ministry to a Vital Generation*. Herndon, VA: Alban Institute, 2010.

———. *Tribal Church: Ministering to the Missing Generation*. Herndon, VA: Alban Institute, 2007.

NORC. "General Social Survey." http://www.norc.org/Research/Projects/Pages/general-social-survey.aspx.

Passel, Jeffrey S., and D'Vera Cohn. "US Population Projections 2005–2050." Washington DC: Pew Hispanic Center, 2008.

Pew Research Center. "America's Changing Religious Landscape." http://www.pewforum.org/2015/05/12/americas-changing-religious-landscape/.

———. "'Nones' on the Rise." http://www.pewforum.org/2012/10/09/nones-on-the-rise/.

———. "Millenials in Adulthood." http://www.pewsocialtrends.org/2014/03/07/millennials-in-adulthood/.

Plekon, Michael. *Living Icon, Hidden Holiness: Saints as They Really Are*. Notre Dame, IN: University of Notre Dame Press, 2012.

Public Religion Research Institute. "I Know What You Did Last Sunday." http://publicreligion.org/research/2014/05/aapor-2014/.

Putnam, Robert D. *Bowling Alone*. New York: Touchstone/Simon & Schuster, 2001.

———. *Our Kids*. New York: Simon & Schuster, 2015.

Putnam, Robert D., and David E. Campbell. *American Grace*. New York: Simon & Schuster, 2010.

Scott, Emily M. "We've Seen Megachurch. But How About Micro-Church?" http://www.huffingtonpost.com/rev-emily-m-d-scott/weve-seen-megachurch-but-_b_5474319.html?ncid=fcbklnkushpmg00000051.

Taylor, Barbara Brown. *An Altar in the World*. San Francisco: HarperSanFrancisco, 2008.

————. *Leaving Church.* San Francisco: HarperSanFrancisco, 2007.

Taylor, Charles. *A Secular Age.* Cambridge: Harvard University Press, 2007.

Walford, Malcolm L., ed. *The Spirit's Tether.* Herndon VA: Alban, 2011.

Wheeler, Barbara. "The Problems with Lay Pastors." *The Christian Century* 127.14 (2010) 28–33.

Wood, Lawrence. "Called But Not Ordained." *The Christian Century* 127.14 (2010) 22–27.

2

From Bonaventure to BustedHalo®: Ministry beyond the Church Walls

—*Brett C. Hoover*

I AM A MEMBER of a vanishing people in U.S. Catholicism—the children of the full-service Catholic parish. The church historian E. Brooks Hollifield speaks of the role of the *social congregation* in American religious history, that is, the local church as a center for all kinds of activities besides worship.[1] Growing up, almost all of the people I knew were parishioners at our large Southern California parish, St. Bonaventure. I attended St. Bonaventure School through the eighth grade, as did my siblings. My mother headed up the fashion show fundraiser for the school one year, and another year she was school chairwoman, that is, lead volunteer. At the church, I sang in the children's choir at the 9 A.M. Sunday Mass, and we rehearsed during school hours once a week in the afternoon. I was an altar boy, including sometimes for the Neo-Catechumenal Way, a para-ecclesial movement based at the parish (my mother belonged). Both my brother and I joined the parish troop of cub scouts. As a teenager, I was a part of the youth ministry group, and I ushered at the evening youth Mass. Even after I left home to attend a state university, my mother helped out with adult initiation of new Catholics, and my father sang in the adult choir.

Given the fact that my family spent so much time on the parish campus, as a young person I surely would have found it difficult to imagine the church "leaving the building." We were practitioners of what Robert Wuthnow calls a *spirituality of dwelling*: "A spirituality of dwelling emphasizes *habitation*: God occupies a definite place in the universe and creates a sacred space in which humans too can dwell; to inhabit sacred

---

1. Hollifield, "Toward a History of American Congregations," 38–43.

space is to know its territory and to feel secure."[2] Growing up, I certainly thought of God's presence as secured whenever I spent time in the sanctified space of the parish church (especially near the tabernacle where the eucharistic bread was reserved for the sick), or when I participated in sacramental life, or marked the great occasions of the liturgical calendar. For Wuthnow, dwelling spirituality is an expression of Durkheim's notion of religion as a bounded, orienting, collective experience as located in a community gathered in a particular physical space.[3] At St. Bonaventure, I simply presumed that our common experience of parish life was life as it ought to be. People outside that orbit might be good people, but they felt less substantial somehow.

Robert Wuthnow, of course, contrasts this dwelling spirituality with the spirituality of seekers—the post-1950s, American experience of the spiritual journey as a constant, personal negotiation of discrete, fleeting experiences of the sacred.[4] The central idea of this volume—of church beyond the building—must be regarded as an expression of seeking spirituality. "Leaving the building" itself is a verbal meme straight from popular culture; its roots are in Elvis Presley concerts of the 1950s, when hall managers would announce that "Elvis has left the building" in order to calm the riotous crowd of young people within. The phrase's adaptation to the ecclesial world, however, comes more recently from the emergent church movement (ECM), a small but influential force within evangelical Christianity in the United States that worries that Christian churches have focused their attention on structure and stability in a way unsuitable to a postmodern world of fluidity and mobility.[5] While Roman Catholics and evangelicals have generally found themselves on opposite sides of ecclesial questions, a dovetailing of increasing evangelical interest in liturgy and monasticism and Catholic concern about departing young adults have created a climate where Roman Catholics have begun to join in emergent church conversations.[6]

Of course, American evangelicals have always had a loose relationship with formal structure and geographical place. Most evangelical churches are resolutely congregational in polity, and many scholars today trace

2. Wuthnow, *After Heaven*, 3–4.

3. Ibid., 3–5.

4. Ibid.

5. Martí and Ganiel, *The Deconstructed Church*, 5–11.

6. See, for example, Kwon, "Catholics Join Emerging Church Conversation," and McKnight, "Five Streams of the Emerging Church."

evangelicalism back to the Second Great Awakening's camp meeting revivals. Catholics, on the other hand, have a historically strong relationship with structure and place. Our parishes have geographical boundaries and belong to a local church (diocese) named after a particular city; our worship is structured and liturgical; our theology of Christian commitment is doggedly communal. True, post-Vatican II Catholicism is shot through with the seeker spirituality upon which the ECM stands. My own geographically-centered experience of Catholicism growing up took place within a functional cavern of a modernist church complete with folk-art stations of the cross. I witnessed countless personal testimonies of faith at retreats and in small group settings. I attended Mass on the beach and confessed my sins in a face-to-face confession more like a dialogue over my distinct spiritual journey than a cataloguing of personal faults. Seeking itself was not unfamiliar to me, just the idea of needing to leave the building to do it.

So is there really room in Roman Catholicism for a portable experience of church? Can the Catholic *ekklesia* leave the building? I would argue that it can, and in fact it *must*. In the Acts of the Apostles, we hear about the power of worship within the early Christian community. "When they had prayed, the place in which they were gathered together was shaken" (Acts 4:31). But that very experience sent them boldly forth into the world in mission. Vatican II's *Gaudium et Spes* insisted that the faithful had to leave the building to do good in the world. It began, "The joys and the hopes, the griefs and the anxieties of the people of this age, especially those who are poor or in any way afflicted, these are the joys and hopes, the griefs and anxieties of the followers of Christ" (*Gaudium et Spes* 1). In fact, the history of Roman Catholicism is replete with examples of people who joyfully moved beyond the church walls to witness *ad extra* to the Christian faith they had experienced powerfully within them—from Lorenzo Ruiz of Manila to Dorothy Day of New York to Mother Teresa of Calcutta. Catholics have founded innumerable social institutions through history and across the world. These hospitals, schools, orphanages, and hospices for the dying arose in response to the passionate faith of a community of the baptized— often women and men in religious communities. They have provided a social safety net for whole societies, not just for Catholics. According to *Forbes* magazine, Catholic Charities is the third largest charitable organization in the United States, after the United Way and the Salvation Army.[7]

---

7. Barrett, "The Largest U.S. Charities for 2012."

Even so, many Catholics sitting in their pews find it difficult to think outside the church. Popular books on the "mission-driven church" stand out precisely because so many cannot imagine such a thing.[8] In my recent life as a parish researcher, I have seen Catholics resist sharing their faith in any public manner, worried they might be mistaken for aggressive proselytizers. I have heard some Catholic parishioners explicitly argue against solidarity with the struggles of immigrants, even though their own ancestors were immigrants. One multi-parish research project brought me to the startling conclusion that, for many urban parishes in one Midwestern city, keeping the building heated, repaired, and open had essentially become the mission of the faith community. In a very real sense, church had been swallowed up by the building. And Catholics also have the bad habit of fetishizing the Sunday liturgy to such an extent that we do not easily see it as having a connection to our trinitarian God's mission to visit and transform all creation. A young woman once waxed nostalgically to me about her former parish, how liturgy there pushed people to bring their experience of communion with God into the world to do good there. "Here," she complained looking around, "the Mass is the thing."

But this sort of liturgical isolationism is not the heart of the problem. Ecclesial inertia has more sociological than theological roots. Sociologist Jerome Baggett has aptly summarized the research. On average, American Catholic parishes are much larger than their Orthodox or Protestant counterparts, and the resulting diffusion of responsibility seems to result in lower contribution rates, less volunteering for the church, and reduced political participation in comparison to other religious groups. Over the last few decades, involved parishioners at Catholic parishes have famously drifted right on the political spectrum, and this conservatism also moves Catholics away from the activist stance of Catholic social teaching. Finally, *institutional differentiation* dilutes ordinary Catholics' sense of ecclesial responsibility. Despite a renewed emphasis on the baptismal priesthood at Vatican II, many defer to clergy and to religious sisters as the authentic ecclesial agents. Other trained professionals—teachers, social workers, hospital personnel—do the daily work of the church's social institutions. The rest of us go to Mass at our local parish and keep the commandments

8. For example, Brennan, *The Mission Driven*, and Rivers, *From Maintenance to Mission*.

at home. Most could scarcely imagine themselves as somehow accountable for the mission of the church beyond the pew.[9]

As a result, when church does leave the building, it usually requires a push. Some person or group of people has to inspire and initiate the move and to invite and challenge others to get involved. My own formation in seminary included substantial reflection on the connection between faith and justice, and even as a young parish priest I knew this ought to be part of parish life. Yet I did little about this until a local rabbi, himself an employee of a labor organization, invited me to get involved in labor campaigns for the sake of marginalized service workers. I ended up working with an interreligious coalition of clergy advocating for the rights of farm workers, hotel workers, and home health care workers. I recall on one occasion that we met with the owner of a large, family-owned supermarket chain, and we asked him to put pressure on a larger produce supplier so that they would be forced to negotiate with the United Farm Workers regarding the conditions of workers picking strawberries. The supermarket owner was skeptical, but he was also Roman Catholic and sympathetic to workers' rights. At the meeting, the rabbi urged me to talk to him about Catholic social teaching on the rights of workers. I began by introducing some of the comments the U.S. Catholic bishops made on behalf of workers. The owner interrupted me and declared, "I don't care what the bishops say, Father. I want to know what you think." I put down my text, and we began to talk. He ended up applying some of the pressure we had hoped he would. Yet it is doubtful that I would have found myself in a position to urge that without the invitation and encouragement of my rabbi colleague.

I do find that leaving the building has a snowballing effect, however. Inertia begins to break down. After I reported about labor activities in a sermon one day, a parishioner—a recent convert to Catholicism—confronted me briskly about this unsavory combining of politics and religion. This time a command of Catholic social teaching did come in handy, and I explained to this parishioner—an executive headhunter with decidedly anti-union views—the long history of popes and bishops defending the rights of workers. I am not sure this changed her mind, but she did admit that it had not occurred to her that the church might be interested and involved in such a stance. And I began to reflect on the social consciousness of our community of parishioners. I worried that we did not make much of a connection between the faith we celebrated together at liturgy and the

9. Baggett, *Sense of the Faithful*, 179–82.

mission it called us to outside the walls. The pastor and several parishio-ners, it turned out, were also concerned. One of them was a friend who had been a social activist in college back home in London; she found herself often surprised at American Catholics' political apathy. With the pastor's encouragement, she and I gathered a handful of parishioners to establish a fledgling social justice committee for the parish. That committee in turn embarked on a month-long educational campaign around Catholic social teaching. The committee continued through my friend and another priest after I had left the parish.

A more unusual way I participated in church leaving the building also came about through an invitation I received that snowballed into a project that continued to grow long after I had departed. This time the invitation came from the president of the religious community of priests to which I belonged at the time, the Paulist Fathers (I have since left in order to marry). Concerned that our community could do more to promote ecclesial out-reach to young adults, Fr. Frank DeSiano decided to gather a focus group of priests from our community, young adults, and various other clergy and lay people involved in young adult ministry. We met in late 1999 around a large table in the basement of the president's house in Jamaica, Queens. The diverse group agreed that the most pressing need was for Catholic outreach on the internet. At that time, the majority of Catholic websites had an ultra-conservative oeuvre. Preaching to the converted, they employed medieval Scholastic theological language and presented a narrow and rigid under-standing of orthodox Catholic teaching. We hoped for something more inviting, more dialogical, with a focus on young people's real questions and dilemmas. We wanted to reach not only the young people already involved in the church but those who were spiritual seekers as well.

Some months after the gathering, DeSiano hired one of the leaders of our parish's young adult group, a radio producer named Mike Hayes, to help create the new website. Then he came to me and asked me to work with Mike. The two of us spent the next year and a half working with a team of media specialists—Sue Donovan, Jeanean Merkel, and Father Larry Rice—and we finally created an innovative website that we thought young people would actually use. To do so, we surveyed young adults online, recorded the observations of focus groups across the country, and tested our initial designs. We ended up creating a large site with two broad subsections—a mildly irreverent set of catechetical resources entitled FaithGuides (writ-ten almost entirely without religious jargon) and an upbeat electronic magazine written by a group of young writers from diverse backgrounds and different parts of the country. FaithGuides included Bible Boot Camp, Mass Class, Prayer Pilot, the Question Box, and an interfaith religious trivia game called Dante's Trivia Inferno, in which an elevator deposited you in heaven, hell, or purgatory depending on your score. Regarding the magazine half, we formed a stable of writers in the vision of what we hoped to accomplish—they attended writers' conferences in New York City where our offices were located—and then we gave them a great deal of latitude. They wrote candidly about nearly every topic imaginable—doubt in the face of personal suffering, sexuality and dating, divorce among twenty-somethings, television and popular music, the war in Iraq. Discussion boards provided forums for people to discuss these articles and whatever else they wanted to talk about. The site went live in late 2001. A young adult group from a Latino parish in the Bronx gave us the site's moniker, BustedHalo.com. They had conceived it as a joke, but young people liked the way it celebrated the imperfect humanity of all of us. The name stuck.

We marketed BustedHalo through ecclesial channels—campus ministry networks, church publications, young adult ministry conferences, and World Youth Day (where we gave out temporary tattoos). BustedHalo began to grow a fan base among both young people already involved in church and the people who worked with them. But we also announced the site's arrival in more secular locations. We advertised in the online edition of the satirical newspaper *The Onion* and on the online charity The Hunger Site. We did guerilla marketing at the Head of the Charles Regatta in Massachusetts. We wanted to move as far outside the church as we could go, and we largely succeeded. Thousands of people with little or no connection to Catholicism visited the site and liked it. Such a foray beyond the church walls did not sit well with everyone. A small group of traditionalist Catholics began to attack visitors who wandered too far from orthodox teaching in their questions or opinions. They chased some of the spiritual-but-not-religious away, and we ended up having to close down the discussion board for a month to prevent their coup d'état from succeeding. A talk show host reported us to the Paulist president for permitting a young married woman to reflect on the issue of birth control, and the online edition of a conservative Catholic magazine stereotyped us as leftist, in part because in one column I had admitted to a mild dislike of Ronald Reagan in my youth. Yet many traditional Catholics liked the verve and openness of the site.

I left BustedHalo after a few years in order to pursue a doctorate in theology, but after my departure the venture continued to grow. Web 1.0 gave way to the social media content of Web 2.0, and new leadership introduced podcasting, internet video, blogging (including a relationships column entitled Pure Sex, Pure Love), celebrity faith interviews, social media pages, and a series of street interviews. The latter included a segment wherein a priest named Father Jack Collins chronicled the creative, ridiculous, and profound answers young people gave to religious questions in various picturesque locations in New York City. The segment was called "You Don't Know Jack" in homage to its host. Another Paulist priest, Father Dave Dwyer, began hosting a satellite radio program, the BustedHalo Show, on Sirius/XM radio. BustedHalo had gone from website to new media platform. Church had wandered beyond the pews into cyberspace and beyond.

But back when I was an usher at St. Bonaventure, I could scarcely have imagined such a thing. Of course, at that time the internet did not exist (except perhaps in Al Gore's brain). And growing up as I did in a suburban, middle-class bubble, I had little knowledge or appreciation for workers' rights and could not have imagined advocating for them as a ministry. But even if I had known more about the struggles of service workers then, even if the internet had existed, I had still grown up assuming that ministry had to do with what occurred on a church campus. After all, even when we "left the building" to go on retreats or do service, we inevitably ended up at some church facility—a church-run soup kitchen or a retreat house operated by a religious order. Even when we struck off to celebrate Mass on the beach—surely a mark of leaving the building if there ever was one—we essentially brought church with us, including all the accoutrements of a traditional mass, though perhaps a little stripped down (I remember at least one priest in his shorts wearing his alb and stole). We could not really escape the bubble of our full-service parish.

Of course, socio-economic bubbles like the one I grew up in still exist, and the more privileged among my undergraduate students at a Jesuit university still show evidence of having inhabited them. But almost none of them know anything about the kind of full-service church environment I have described here. In fact, increasingly my students have little knowledge or experience of church life at all. This, after all, is the generation where almost a third describe themselves as having no religion.[10] And a disproportionate share of these so-called "nones" live in the Western United States,

10. Funk and Smith, "'Nones' on the Rise," 10.

where our university is located.[11] Even those among my students who do attend church on a regular or semi-regular basis are not greatly defined by that act. They also bring stories of having attended different churches, synagogues, or mosques with some frequency. They have many influential friends not of their own religion. They even perform many of the activities traditionally associated with church—like social service—through public schools or nonprofit organizations unrelated to religion. In short, unlike me, they have spent most of their lives outside church buildings.

They also think of faith (or spirituality, as they often prefer) in individualistic terms, as a personal journey. In Wuthnow's language, they are resolutely seekers, not dwellers. Many do not even think of church as a reasonable place to go to seek the sacred or the transcendent. They look for God in nature or in the heartfelt conversation between friends. They may even expect to find the holy in meditation or prayer, but not in church. When I speak about church with my students, the first thing that comes to mind for many is boredom. On the one hand, I often think in response that a little boredom might do this generation, which has come of age in a world of computer games and smartphones, some good. On the other hand, how many times have I agreed? Church can indeed be downright boring. At the same time, I am far from ready to give it up, and I hope that at least some of my students will eventually have a taste of the profound experiences of community and spiritual depth I have found sitting in my pew. But they will not find their way there on their own. In other words, leaving the church building may simply be the price we must pay if we religious people wish to speak with the younger generation about spiritual things. Not long ago I was at a church event dominated by people over sixty-five, and a woman turned around and exclaimed how good it was to have young people present. My wife—then my fiancée—reminded her that she was looking at two people in their forties. That event sticks in my mind. I fear that if church does not leave the building, we may soon find that there is nobody there but us old folks.

Bibliography

Baggett, Jerome. *Sense of the Faithful: How American Catholics Live Their Faith.* New York: Oxford University Press, 2009.

Barrett, William P. "The Largest U.S. Charities for 2012." *Forbes* (November 8, 2012). http://www.forbes.com/sites/williampbarrett/2012/11/08/the-largest-u-s-charities-for-2012/.

11. Ibid., 21.

Brennan, Patrick J. *The Mission Driven Parish*. Maryknoll, NY: Orbis, 2007.

Hollifield, E. Brooks. "Toward a History of American Congregations." In *New Perspectives in the History of Congregations,* vol. 2 of *American Congregations,* edited by James P. Wind and James L. Lewis, 23–53. Chicago: University of Chicago Press, 1994.

Funk, Cary, and Greg Smith. "'Nones' on the Rise: One-in-Five Adults Have No Religious Affiliation." Washington, DC: Pew Research Center, 2012.

Kwon, Lillian. "Catholics Join Emerging Church Conversation." *The Christian Post* (March 13, 2009). http://www.christianpost.com/news/catholics-join-emerging-church-conversation-37481.

Martí, Gerardo, and Gladys Ganiel. *The Deconstructed Church: Understanding Emerging Christianity*. New York: Oxford University Press, 2014.

McKnight, Scot. "Five Streams of the Emerging Church." *Christianity Today* (January 19, 2007). http://www.christianitytoday.com/ct/2007/february/11.35.html/.

Rivers, Robert S. *From Maintenance to Mission: Evangelization and the Revitalization of the Parish*. New York: Paulist, 2005.

Wuthnow, Robert. *After Heaven: Spirituality in the United States since the* 1950s. Berkeley: University of California Press, 1998.

3

The Church Has Left—and
Should Leave?—the Building

—Adam A. J. DeVille

OVER THE COURSE OF the last decade, I have been thinking about church communities and church buildings in several quite distinct contexts, from Canadian Anglicans to American Amish to Ukrainian Catholics. Let me start with the Anglicans in southern Ontario, among whom I grew up.[1]

Around the autumn of 2005, I felt a great sadness when I visited home only to discover that my paternal family's parish church—of which my grandfather was first warden, on whose first roof my own father worked as a young boy in the early 1950s, and to whose ongoing life my paternal family contributed so much for half a century—was gone. No natural disaster had befallen it; neither fire nor wind nor water had destroyed it. It was voluntarily deconsecrated, deconstructed, and then deleted from the memory of the neighborhood. The entire edifice was torn down, the land sold, and on that substantial corner lot in a leafy and comfortably established subdivision there now stand two or three homogenous homes in that boring cookie-cutter style beloved of developers with more avarice than imagination.

The Anglican Church of St. Stephen, Brantford, Ontario, Canada's first (it was claimed) "Coronation Church" (opened in 1953, when Elizabeth II was crowned, but actually started earlier) is, at least in worldly eyes, something that never existed. The innocent passerby would never know what had stood on that lot previously; no marker tells the story of a community of faith that, for fifty years, stood there to love, pray, and grow together.

I had known, to be sure, that the parish, like many, had fallen on hard times; I had known from my parents that there was talk about closing this

1. Parts of this essay originally appeared as "The Worthy Patrimony of Anglicanism," in *Crosstalk*, the official paper of the Anglican Diocese of Ottawa, in October 2006.

parish; and I had even heard from them that the deed had been done and the building sold. But nothing quite prepared me for the shock of driving down the street and seeing not even the slightest trace of the former building but instead three suburban houses in their smug newness, pretending for all the world that nothing else so pretty or so important had ever existed there.

That story, alas, has been replicated many times in southern Ontario and elsewhere, and not merely among Anglicans but Christians of all traditions—Protestant, Catholic, and Orthodox. The loss of a beloved building was brought home to me again more recently. In April of 2014, St. Elias the Prophet Ukrainian Greek Catholic Church in Brampton, Ontario, where my wife and I were crowned in marriage, burned to the ground in a few hours. Thanks to Facebook and Twitter feeds, we were able, living in northern Indiana, to watch it disappear before our eyes. It was an enormous shock to many people. As I adjusted to the news, the verse about "For here we have no lasting city" (Heb 13:14) came back to mind as I reflected on the tension that Christians live with: to be citizens of a particular country, while having our ultimate allegiance elsewhere; to be embodied creatures worshipping an incarnate God who nonetheless transcends us and our buildings; to be people who can be edified by worshipping in beautiful, icon-drenched cathedrals with gold chalices—or in a bed in a barracks at night in a Siberian gulag using a broken spoon to hold hardened, stale crumbs of bread for the Eucharist. What, then, ought to be our relationship to buildings, and the relationship between the church and churches, that is between the mystical body of Christ and the ways in which we manifest that?

I have no tidy answers here, but I want to reflect on three other ways of being the church, all outside of church buildings. Since 2007 I have lived surrounded by Amish in Northern Indiana. At first I knew nothing of them other than their ubiquitous buggies on the road. But I have since read much about them and watched several documentaries, and gotten to know a few of them from whom we buy almost all our vegetables, fruits, and plants at a splendid nearby market they run. They have no church buildings. They worship every second week in a member's home, and that home rotates from month to month. Worship usually begins in the morning, and goes on for several hours, followed by an equally lengthy community feast. It's an all-day affair on alternate Sundays; the "off" Sundays are for quieter, simpler worship *en famille*.

When the local community gets too big for everyone to gather in one home for worship, then the community is divided and one half is sent away to start a new settlement in another nearby but under-served area. Thus they keep their communities to a size where people can know one another well. I have to say that I find this model deeply attractive and if I could get over my Byzantine liturgical snobbery, as well as a few other theological and sacramental issues with Amish theology, I would be tempted to join them. (The thought of abandoning most modern technology bothers me far less than the theological issues. I despise cell phones, leaf blowers, clothes dryers, and the constant distracting whirligig that is the Internet, and would gladly go back to communicating via hand-written letter, using a collection of wonderful fountain pens a deceased friend left me several years ago.)

My attraction to an Amish life is not, I hasten to add, a species of romanticism or nostalgia for a past that never truly was. Nor, despite my little rant above, am I really a Luddite. My attraction to the Amish comes, I suspect, from seeing them live on a life-long basis a form of community I had for only a few years, but would so very gladly and keenly take up again.

For the last half of the 1990s, I lived in an ecumenical community in Ottawa. We were all working students at the time, most of us beginning grad school while also teaching or working part-time. We had met through our Anglican parish of the Ascension and all felt a longing for more than just Sunday worship. Through many months of getting together for Bible study, discussion groups, cycling and later jogging along the Rideau Canal, or backyard summer parties lubricated with plenty of sangria and good food, we discovered that we wanted to try an experiment in "intentional community" as we called it. (Part of our initial vision came from what we had heard about Sojourners communities in Washington, DC.) So the five of us—three men and two women—decided to take a chance for a year. As providence would have it, we found the most amazing apartment together right downtown, on the corner of a major intersection, and it was called Somerset House. It had, in the early twentieth century, once been a long-term hotel and, just possibly, a brothel also—we could never quite conclude how apocryphal that tale was, but the evidence seemed likely that Edwardian madams had plied their trade there once! True or not, we liked to scandalize our mothers and other overly genteel visitors with that tale when they came to visit for the first time.

The owners had long since renovated the top two floors into a unique space: a two-floor apartment with three bathrooms, four bedrooms, living and dining rooms, large foyer, small library, rooftop deck, and the most wonderfully massive and elaborately-equipped kitchen I've ever had the joy to work in (as a Michelin chef *manqué*, I still dream lustfully of recreating that kitchen in my own home someday if I win the lottery). Beneath our apartment was a Spanish tapas bar with live flamenco music, a more sedate old English pub, and a rather dodgier establishment where bearded bikers played billiards until odd hours. We were thrilled to find such a place and more thrilled to be able to afford it. We pooled money together for meals in common and other household expenses and it quickly became a hospitable place for all kinds of friends and family to gather. Two of my roommates began, shortly after we moved in, to work on a project for urban gardening with a run-down poor neighborhood a few blocks from where we lived, and in short order BUGS ("Byetown Urban Gardens"[2]) was born and took off, allowing people, some with no gardening experience and little income, their first chance to grow their own food.

We were an eclectic lot—a Calvinist feminist, two recovering Baptists, a Dutch Reformed, and me, the cradle Anglican of the lot (who became Catholic part-way through my time there, adding enormously to the challenges of our theological engagements, which simultaneously became more difficult and more interesting). We disagreed on many things. Some of the group started out as vegetarians, but we quickly showed them the error of their ways. We did so amicably and I am happy to say I have remained friends with all who lived there, even though we've all long since departed. The building itself partially collapsed a few years ago and is now uninhabitable. We got off to a rocky start when, within two weeks of moving in, I was hit by a bus while riding my bike (the driver being totally at fault) and spent three months in hospital, and then the better part of a year undergoing therapy to learn to walk again. My friends were wonderful in not only letting my mother sleep in my room while she visited me at the hospital for several weeks, but in coming to rescue me with homemade soup and bread from the ghastly slop then passing for food in the hospital.

I stayed in Somerset House for four years, but after the first year, two people left to go overseas on a mission trip, and others to attend school elsewhere. But each new lot of people became fast friends and it was a great experience of being challenged to live Christianity, not just an hour on Sunday, but every day. We challenged each other to practice hospitality among ourselves, but also with the homeless people who lived on our street. We quickly learned that it's very easy to smile and chat cheerfully over coffee

---

2. "Byetown" was Ottawa's original name before Queen Victoria chose it to be the national capital.

after Sunday liturgy for a few minutes, but the challenges to cheerfulness and charity alike become more acute when one roommate consistently fails to replace the toilet paper, or doesn't cough up for the grocery fund that week, or invites house-guests whom you would like to defenestrate. Then the façade of piety gives way and you see if you have any real patience underneath or not. The learning was sometimes difficult, sometimes painful, but even at moments of acute tension, we somehow managed to pray together, put up with one another, and patiently work through the conflict and anger so as to never lose sight of the humanity of the other person, and the Christian call to love no matter what.

Let me reflect, finally, on another, much briefer, experience of "intentional community" in Tempe, Arizona in 2006 while visiting a friend who was then for a time involved in the City of the Lord, a large community born out of the charismatic movement in the Catholic Church following Vatican II. Many of them bought houses around their local Catholic parish, and have since tightly intertwined their lives. When my friend, his wife and two kids, and elderly parents first moved into this community early in the last decade, they had thirty people on their lawn within an hour unpacking the truck, scrubbing toilets, bringing them food, and doing many other things—a pattern that was completely commonplace for that community. If someone was sick, or a family member died, you immediately had all kinds of unsought help—from casseroles to prayers to babysitting to just sitting and listening. Though I had (and have) no stomach for their charismatic worship, the level of very real, practical service to and support of one another in this community deeply impressed me. They had buildings—a parish church and individual homes—but much of their community transcended the physical places, and they refused to retreat into individualistic lives once leaving the parking lot after Mass on Sunday.

How often, even after being married for more than a decade, have I wanted to recreate these forms of community! I desire to do so *not* because of any fault or lack in my wife and children, whom I dearly love and from whom I have been incalculably blessed. But spouse and children cannot, and should not, be one's only community. (As Stanley Hauerwas reminded us many years ago now, the gospel is very hard on "family values" if they are used to the exclusion of the stranger, the suffering, and even of God.) Here I return to some of the reading I did in the 1990s, particularly from spiritual writers such as Henri Nouwen and Jean Vanier, both of whom argued that the great loneliness of many people in modern mass industrialized societies, where we all pick up and regularly move to chase economic fortunes across the continent and sometimes the world, means that we are rootless and community-less, and often love-less as a result. The truth is, when God says it is not good for the human person to be alone, he didn't mean that one solitary spouse would suffice. As every Christian tradition today realizes, the human "being as communion" (to borrow John Zizioulas' famous phrase) is what God intended—communion in families, yes, but with other human beings, the world, and with God.

Zizioulas' theological vision is a grand and compelling one, which goes some distance to explaining the widespread use of *Being as Communion* in Catholic, Protestant, and Orthodox seminaries and universities. But how are we to live that in practice? Are any of the models noted above something for Christians to consider anew on a much wider scale, demographic challenges and changes or not? Can we—should we?—be more like the Amish, or the City of the Lord, or Somerset House? Whether we want to or not, it seems that in many places if communities of faith are going to survive, they will have to do so outside of buildings, which are fast disappearing. Perhaps, then, we are returning to the age of the house churches.

I am not, to be sure, advocating an extreme version of congregationalist ecclesiology here—American Protestantism on steroids where in addition to the 33,000 denominations currently afloat, we add infinitely more by every one of us feeling authorized to start a church at home. I have, in fact, no simple or tidy answers. But it does seem to me that for some time now there has been a real gap between churches and communities: the former have long been cavernous gathering-halls for hundreds (and now, in the era of "mega-churches," thousands) to meet their liturgical obligations and sacramental needs, but they have not been the latter. Churches, that is, have rarely supplied a sense of close-knit community along the lines of the Amish or some of the other examples noted above. Especially in large urban, and particularly Roman Catholic, parishes, it is possible to be a complete and total stranger, isolated and alone, even after years of faithful Sunday attendance. Some people prefer it that way, and are entitled to do so, but I know many ex-Catholics among my students who tell me that they decamped for a different church because people there knew their names, called when they were sick, and took an interest in them personally.

Are there ways, then, for Christians to deepen local community roots today even in large metropolitan centers? Are there ways that parishes of high liturgical life—especially Catholic and Orthodox—can keep the liturgics but ground it in much closer, more caring community, perhaps along Amish lines? Some parishes, I know, have experimented with such groups through various parish renewal programs over the years or by means of Lenten Bible studies at home, but these are all *ad hoc* and short-lived affairs, and when they are over, we all go back to our rather atomistic lives. What I think we need are long-term, stable, close-knit communities, membership in which is really very much expected if not required.

How do we set those up? Are they even possible given today's socio-economic strictures? (In my more despairing moments, I think the great moral philosopher Alasdair MacIntyre is right: the problem is less with the church and much more with "that dangerous and unmanageable institution," the modern nation-state, about which we can do very little it seems.) Would they not run the very real danger of becoming mechanisms of control and abuse? These questions admit of no easy answers, but I think they are crucial questions today and we are past the time when we could ignore them.

To some extent, Eastern parishes (both Catholic and Orthodox) may once have had an advantage here and not realized it. Historically at least the ethnic makeup of such parishes may have been a strength and not a weakness. But even in such parishes I have seen the effects of today's socioeconomic changes pressing deeply on them, sending many members far and wide for schooling and employment, and attenuating the bonds between the remaining members thanks to the pressures of North American individualism and the repugnant crony capitalism we see on display so often. So there are no safe havens, and nobody has any grounds for being smug. We all have some hard thinking to do to be prepared for being more deeply in communion with one another and with God in different ways as this century continues to unfold.

4

The Home that Joy Built

—*Maria Gwyn McDowell*

O heavenly King, Comforter, the Spirit of truth, who are everywhere and fill all things, Treasury of Blessings and Giver of life, come and abide in us. Cleanse us of every impurity, and save our souls, O Good One.

—Orthodox Daily Prayers

The beginning of love is the will to let those we love be perfectly themselves, the resolution not to twist them to fit our own image. If in loving them we do not love what they are, but only their potential likeness to ourselves, then we do not love them: we only love the reflection of ourselves we find in them.

—Thomas Merton, *No Man Is an Island*

***

FOR AS LONG AS I can remember, the church has been my building, my home, my *ekklesia*. Its sounds, sights, and smells—no matter where I heard, saw, or smelled them—would assemble themselves around me, as if I were there, as if I were touching its walls, kneeling on its rugs, kissing its icons.

Always. Still. It is my home. It just isn't necessarily *there* anymore.

***

Balanced precariously with the older kids on the steps to the altar, I watched our priest describe his vestments. The cords to the cuffs were so long! At five or six years old, I didn't understand, but I remember that each item meant *something*. I remember wanting to understand.

34

A few years later the same priest came to find me and my friend. He walked us past the people hanging icons on the bare walls, unrolling rugs across empty floors, reassembling stands for music, icons, and candles. "I want to show you the altar," gesturing us in. He took us around all three sides of the altar, showing the table of preparation, the menorah-like candlestick, the place where the altar boys stored the processional items. He described everything on the altar table. I was enthralled. I remember him saying, "I want you to see this now, before you aren't allowed in here anymore."

As a teen, my Sunday School teachers asked us to memorize John 3:16. This seemed like a very nice verse to pick. (I knew nothing about the particular Protestant fascination with this text.) Our teachers challenged us to find the verse in the liturgy. I listened for it, avidly. There it was! Tucked away in the prayers the priest said quietly while preparing Communion. For the first time, it occurred to me that the liturgy is full of Scripture. I was intrigued.

Intrigued enough that at summer camp, I looked forward to the extra assignments, usually in the form of knowledge scavenger hunts, searching from icon to book and back again. Peter was a few years older than me. He was nice enough, popular with everyone at camp. I wasn't so sure about him since he teased me about my curiosity when the priests weren't around, but he sure seemed eager when they were around. We both asked questions, we both shared what we knew, and the priests—they liked our interest, our enthusiasm, our curiosity. Everyone said he would make a good priest.

When I was thinking about college, I told a friendly priest that I was interested in seminary. I wasn't sure why. I just knew that was where you went to learn about church and God. I wondered what he thought. He said I should go to college first.

I chose my college in part because it was in a city full of Orthodox churches. Somehow I missed that it doesn't matter how many Orthodox churches there are in Los Angeles if you don't have a car. By the end of the first semester, the monthly campus liturgy included me, the priest, his *matushka*, and two young daughters. I returned to college for my second semester, unhappily realizing that I had no church community. The Bible study across the hall that I had been assiduously avoiding suddenly looked more interesting.

It was. I joined an inductive study of the Gospel of Mark and for the first time, intensively studied this person Jesus. I knew all the stories but I hadn't quite understood that Jesus was as interested in challenging injustice as I was, that Jesus wanted the world to change too. Well, to be honest, he was far more interested than I was. He actually did things and got in trouble for it. I was hooked.

I was also growing worried as I realized that Christ was at the center of my Orthodox community *and* this community of Protestants (and a few Catholics). No one had told me that this was possible, and I had the distinct impression that many Orthodox seemed to think it was actually *not* possible. Logically reconciling the clear presence of God *here,* among these people with no building, no icons, no candles, and music that would make my mother cringe, with a God who was supposed to be *there,* was troubling. Nothing I read seemed to allow for *both/and,* especially in the heyday of mass conversions to Orthodoxy that tended to drip with sneering rejection of the converts' immediate, usually Protestant, past.

I was comforted by the daily reminder that the Spirit was everywhere and working in all things. While I knew, having diligently read *The Way of the Pilgrim,* that the Jesus Prayer was supposed to be my prayer without ceasing (my Protestant friends couldn't quite decide what to do with my application of their Pauline striving for constant prayer), for me it had always been the prayer of the Comforter, "everywhere and in all things." I don't remember when it began, I just knew I felt a little guilty that my head always echoed with the wrong prayer, a prayer that now seemed so particularly *right.*

Periodically I found my way to an Orthodox liturgy, borrowing a car and braving the tangle of LA freeways. One Sunday the bishop declared: "The church is here," pointing at the floor. "It is in these walls," gesturing around us at the icons. "The church is *this* building, it is in *these* walls. *This* is where we need to be." I drove home, weeping in frustration as I returned to where I also knew the church to be, outside those walls, away from that building, among those that had never seen an icon, had never smelled incense, and who sang in a pleasantly predicable Western scale.

One day my non-Orthodox friends held a Eucharist on the Thursday before Western Easter. It was one thing to study Scripture and serve the needy with my friends. It was another to take the Eucharist with them. I grew up in an Orthodoxy of frequent Communion where the eucharistic gathering both made us a community, and was the sign of our participation in *the* church. Orthodoxy was the one true church and other churches were *not church.* And yet here, among these people without a building, Christ was present. I chose to receive.

After all, I was a good Orthodox Christian who understood that Eucharist and community are integrally tied. One does not happen without the other. I was participating in the body and blood of Christ surrounded by the body of Christ. Here, *and there*, was the King, the Comforter, the Spirit of truth. I somewhat frantically reminded myself that Orthodox theology declares that we know where the church is, but we don't know where it isn't.

I visited the same priest of my youth and asked him what he thought. He simply offered that by taking Communion outside of the Orthodox Church, I was now "out of communion." I had excommunicated myself.

Over the next nine years, I thrived, grew, and struggled with practices new and strange. At first, I wept almost every night at the loss of my beloved home, the building I loved. Periodic visits only made me feel a stranger. Over time, my grief subsided, becoming as periodic as visits to Orthodox churches.

In seminary I was dubbed a "reluctant Protestant." I did not enter seminary with any intent to seek ordination and chose the shortest degree possible, the MA. I knew perfectly well I was avoiding the MDiv. When I finally switched to the MDiv, I viewed the extra classes as academic gravy. Despite my clear aptitude for preaching, despite my joy at using words to make Scripture and theology engaging and challenging to listeners, despite the consistent positive feedback and the invitation to serve as the homiletics teaching assistant I received, and accepted, from my professor—a female Presbyterian minister—I took my interest in preaching as a proclivity for lecturing and teaching. My pastoral ministry teacher thought I was too theologically-minded for practical ministry. I pushed aside the rebellious thought that perhaps theology and pastoral ministry should be better integrated, a reflection of my Orthodox upbringing. Instead, I happily interpreted this as an indication that I was unsuited to ministry.

Not everyone agreed. I was well-received in my requisite pastoral internship. The supervising pastor said she was a bit taken aback by my certainty that I wasn't called to church ministry, but was hardly going to press me. The supervisor affiliated with my seminary was not so hands-off: she said she was disappointed that I was not seriously considering ordination because the ministry needed women like me. I thanked her, and then ignored her.

I was a puzzle to others and to myself. I openly supported the ordination of women, critiquing Orthodoxy and conservative evangelicalism on this topic, often in the same breath. But I was not interested in pursuing or-dained ministry. I did not quite fit into the models of ministry or of liturgy that surrounded me, and I certainly seemed inclined towards the academic.

Not once, however, did I act on repeated suggestions to visit an Epis-copal church, despite the fact that the Episcopal church across the street from my school was undergoing a revitalization that even the evangelicals knew about (and rejected because, well, it was what later came to be known as an "open and affirming" congregation). Orthodoxy was flooded with former Episcopalians who decried its descent into unorthodoxy and I was less immune to their rhetoric than I wanted to admit. I wasn't quite ready to truck with those who rejected the resurrection (as if Spong actually represented all Episcopalians). I diligently avoided Episcopalians, even my pastoral seminar director, who was a member of that vibrant church across the street, and who I rather liked. I didn't do stuffy English liturgy. I did vaguely chaotic Orthodox liturgy. Period. Besides, every time I glimpsed a woman in clerical collar, my breath caught. Surely I couldn't bear an entire liturgy without breathing!

I wrote my final paper in our series of required systematic theology courses as a personal statement of faith, a bit against my better intellectual judgment. I was not a fan of personal faith statements; I had the Nicene Creed. To my horror, this assignment made it very clear that I was not sim-ply a reluctant Protestant. I was just not very Protestant at all. Somehow, this wild evangelical seminary with over eighty denominations had con-firmed my love for the vibrancy and openness of Orthodox theology. It did not confirm it because those around me failed the test of Orthodoxy, but because what I saw embodied in their lives and practices was the presence of God, of the Spirit who is everywhere and in all things. Orthodox theol-ogy seemed the best expression of what I was seeing, even as so much Or-thodox rhetoric rejected that very possibility. What I missed, what I longed for, what I wept over, was not the absence of the Spirit, but the particular beauty through which the Spirit expressed itself in Orthodox prayer and practice. I left seminary having witnessed the presence of God "everywhere and in all things," in buildings and bodies of unexpected dimensions. The home I wanted, however, was the building which housed the sights, sounds, and smells so distinct to Orthodoxy.

Returning to my home parish after seminary was a struggle. There was no outlet for any pastoral or teaching ministry. Within Orthodoxy, there is no significant understanding of a priesthood of all believers, much less an established practice of sharing ministerial work with the unordained. The few times I shared my thoughts on women and ministry, someone would inevitably find and gently correct me. Or they would relate that, when they were young, they shared my passions, but wisely grew out of such radicalism. I made the priest very uncomfortable: "No one without a degree from an Orthodox school will ever teach or preach as long as I am the priest."

I knew perfectly well that the issue was not a degree, but the fact that I disagreed with commonly accepted practices, that I challenged the status quo regarding women and their roles. As long as I held such belief I would be dismissed, degree or no. Maybe he hoped that seminary would serve as a corrective, maybe it would cure my intransigence. As much as I wished that I could be a contentedly Orthodox woman, considering seminary as a cure felt like drowning.

Apparently, it no longer required a female cleric to stop my breath. During that particular Lent I was acutely aware that by the time I reached the eucharistic cup, I was seething. I wanted to shriek out my frustration at receiving the body in a place where I could not participate in the body in a way that aligned with the gifts of my body. I was unable to discern whether I felt this way because of the circumstances of this particular parish or Orthodoxy itself, but I knew this throat-tightening anger was a problem. I gave myself until Pentecost to sort it out. By Pentecost I realized that I couldn't sort it out in this place, so I left the building. Again.

When I finally decided to pursue a doctorate in theological ethics, I did so fully aware that theology is done from within a praying community. In Orthodoxy, the theologian is one who prays, and prayer is corporate as well as private. In my new city, I found a priest who knew my interests, my beliefs, and welcomed me wholeheartedly into his parish. He offered me the willingness to converse about difficult issues without reactive fear, scolding, or vague dismissals to just be content with all the wonderful things I *could* do in the church. More than that, to the extent that he was permitted within the bounds of acceptability, he gracefully and consistently sought to encourage the fullest possible participation of women and girls of all ages, recognizing and encouraging their gifts. He saw that, like boys, girls can and should be nurtured in their love for all parts of the church and its life, and that love is best nurtured through welcome and participation.

Yet he could not fix the underlying problem: women were excluded for any number of reasons from full participation in the ecclesial life of the church. Even as Orthodox seminaries enroll women, and some in the church make heroic efforts to place these women, such positions are few and far between. Even were they a dime a dozen, some gifts possessed by women simply cannot be exercised with any consistency in the Orthodox Church. Female participation, from reading the epistle, to chanting, to holding the Communion cloth, to teaching, to preaching, is entirely up to the whim of a particular priest in a particular parish, and can change almost without warning.

My point here is not to argue for why this practice of exclusion is actually a failure of Orthodox ecclesiology and theology, not its natural outgrowth. I have done that elsewhere. Rather, it is to speak to its effect: the abrogation of joy, and the failure to love.

I grew up in a church whose theology emphasized joy—in particular, liturgical joy. The liturgical theology of Alexander Schmemann, who taught most of the priests of my youth, was motivated by a relentless pursuit of liturgical joy since "joy is the only really transforming power in the world."[1] But my experience, as a girl-child always outside the altar, gifts passed over for a boy who chided her for sharing his inclinations, was of growing joylessness.

I experienced moments when the liturgy was rich, glorious, and full of joy. Yet my joy lasted only until I looked up from my choir book, or away from a beautiful icon, and my gaze was filled with the *iconostasis*, that barrier I was never allowed to cross except for that once, as a child, before the space it contains was consecrated, made too holy for my female body.

Once I was in a large church with an ample supply of altar servers. Looking up from my music, my eyes widened as I watched thirteen men and boys come out of the deacon doors in exact formation, coming together in the middle, perfectly lined up, candles ablaze as the gospel was a carried out by the priest. All I could think was, "I am watching a phalanx of men" and I could not help but cynically wonder at what point the liturgy became a parade ground for military maneuvers.

Then there was the evening I was chanting the overwhelmingly beautiful and mournful Holy Week burial service, a perfect expression of "sorrowful joy." When the time came for the lights to be lowered, the chanters did what they had always done: they joined the priest in the darkened altar, ready to bear the body of Christ while chanting the funeral hymn. Suddenly I was alone at the chant stand, the only woman chanting that evening. It wasn't that I was any less capable than the men with whom I had just been

1. Schmemann, *For the Life of the World*, 55.

chanting, but that I was a woman and women do not go in the altar during liturgy. When a woman (or even a man) dares to question this custom some defender will patiently point out that only those that are necessary go into the altar. Yet here I was, unnecessary when every male peer was necessary. I was immobilized with horror and shame, unnecessary simply because I was woman.

Others, of course, will point out that it is not that women *per se* are not allowed. After all, nuns enter the altar in their monasteries during the liturgy. These brilliant interlocutors don't seem to notice that the requirements for women to engage in the most basic of liturgical altar service far exceed anything demanded of males, from committed priest to wavering altar boy.

Over and over again, the liturgy reminded me that I was a woman who was not permitted to participate fully alongside my male peers who shared my interests, my gifts, my joy, but not my body. That niggling sadness I had experienced, knowing that I was only allowed to see the contents of the altar because it wasn't yet consecrated, or grief-laced jealousy (quickly suppressed and never admitted to until now) that Peter would get to spend a whole summer being thoughtfully encouraged to consider the priesthood, or the catch in my throat every time I glimpsed a woman in a clerical collar, became insuppressible grief and rage.

I am hardly alone in my struggle. From the work of the theologian Elísabeth Behr-Sigel to the steady trickle of grateful, but almost always private, responses to my online writing, others share my dissatisfaction. A friend once asked me about the topic of my dissertation, and with some hesitancy, I told her. She paused, looked at me, and then looked away. "I have two little girls," she said. "I don't ask those questions because I think the answer might make me really angry." For many frustrated Orthodox, it is better to just not ask.

Women such as me present a serious problem for Orthodoxy. Contemporary Orthodox anthropology posits human persons as unique and irreducible and yet so much contemporary theology reduces men and women to sexed roles which proscribe permissible participation. At the same time, Orthodox theologians argue that joy is nurtured through participation according to the gifts granted to each unique person. When sex-based roles trump gift-based participation, joy is truncated.

Joy-filled participation requires we attend carefully to Merton's recognition that love sees others *as they are*. This is a key component to joy:

recognizing oneself and others as unique and irreducible. Only through such truth-filled recognition can we *relate* in love according to this mutually recognized uniqueness. Otherwise, as Merton says, we love only ourselves, our preferences, our inclinations, our own image.

The repeated irony for me was that *outside* my ecclesial building, *outside* my household, I was competent and capable, a leader who had much to offer her communities. Outside this building, I was recognized as a competent and creative theologian. Within this building, I was accused of misinterpreting my gifts and the gifts of all women. I was accused of refusing to be content with the many other things I could do in the church (few of which actually exercise pastoral or teaching gifts, but that minor detail aside . . .). I was told to fit myself into the image of (presumably) content Orthodox women of every century. I was accused of unbridled arrogance—of believing that my desires, my interests, and my preferences were substantive enough to challenge the church, which has always been this way.

My love for Orthodoxy, for its rich traditions, its beautiful buildings, its dynamic liturgy, its open and generous theology could not be consistently returned in this building, in this space, in this home. Orthodoxy cannot fully love women like me because it cannot even *see* women like me. The insight of a few theologians simply does not outweigh the approbation, confusion, or denial encountered in the ecclesial every-day by those women (and I strongly suspect, some men) who do not fit their appropriately-gendered mold.

This constant denial of the unique giftedness of men and women is a repeated and persistent failure to love, embodied in the very liturgical practices of the church. Such practices fail to encourage the transformation of her and her community into a people able to fully represent God in and to the world.

I am, at this time, no longer participating in an Orthodox church. I left the Orthodox Church because I had to: I was denied Communion because I finally came to deeply love someone who also came to love me. I am now married to her, and we are not welcome to either receive Communion or even attend any of our local Orthodox churches. Few experiences have been more painful than being repeatedly told by more than one priest that I should not come back his church, that I was unwelcome to even set foot in these beloved buildings. There are parishes, in other cities, where we would be welcome, where "don't ask, don't tell" is alive and well, just not in my hometown. I finally went, with my then partner and now wife, to an Episcopal church.

I may have left Orthodoxy because of my choice in partner, but that is not why I cannot return.

For the first time in my life, I am participating in a liturgy that consistently brings joy. This is not to say that I am always satisfied. I will carry my preferences, and sometimes my prejudices, wherever I go. But no longer is worship an exercise in girding up my loins just to survive the service, eking out moments of joy in the midst of a practice that constantly reminded me that my gifts were not welcome because my body could not be imagined by others as the bearer of such gifts.

Joy, as it turns out, is also terribly disconcerting. How strange, that joy should feel this way, that I should be thrown off-balance by the experience of this very thing for which I have so longed. How odd that I should find it odd to love the liturgy without anger, to say the prayers of repentance without feeling that I must defend my very self against the constant perception that I am, myself, *wrong*, that my very desires, my gifts, my joys, are things from which I should turn away. What a relief to be able to see, acknowledge, and repent of my actual sins, not those put upon me by a community that can only form me into its image, not the one given to me by God. How astonishing to look up from my hymnal and see not some of us, but *all* of us. Sometimes it still takes a moment to register that when I look up, I see the embodiment of God's many gifts, freely distributed, joyfully exercised. That moment is disconcerting and the invitation to enter into joy is harder to accept than I wish. It saddens me to realize how much energy I lost to swelling anger, and how hard that habit is to put aside.

I have wished for years that I could simply be someone else: someone willing to accept my place, someone more malleable, more content, who had gifts that were actually welcome. I wanted, almost more than anything else, to be a person who could be joyful in a particular building, in a particular house, in a particular *ekklesia*. Instead, someone else welcomed me into their home.

Now that I have tasted the joy of belonging in a place where I am welcome, where my gifts and passions are sources of delight and interest for others, I cannot imagine returning to a community that refused to see me and other women like me for who we are, for the gifts we can bring.

Joy requires nurture. I may always miss the ancient beauty of Orthodox liturgy. But its beauty is nothing in compare to the beauty of a love that sees, that recognizes, and that encourages the flourishing of each unique and irreducible person. This is the love that makes a building and a people a home, an *ekklesia*. This is the love that nurtures joy.

Bibliography

Merton, Thomas. *No Man is an Island.* Boston: Shambhala, 2000.

Schmemann, Alexander. *For the Life of the World: Sacraments and Orthodoxy.* 2nd rev. and expanded ed. Crestwood, NY: St. Vladimir's Seminary, 1988.

5

"To Not Lose Any Part"

—*Justin Mathews*

I HAVE ALWAYS FELT like a priest on the fringe of the Lord's garment just trying to hold on, especially when around other priests. My short nine years of experience as priest has been a tug of war between an ordained vocation that comes with expectations of "what a priest should be and do" and my personality, my interests, and talents. These often war with each other in my mind, but it shouldn't be so. I have learned to live into and with an uneasy ecclesial existence. It is precisely in the struggle to become a whole man, a priest, that I have experienced the mercy of God and practiced true religion.

I found great solace in reading the introduction to Fr. Alexander Schmemann's journal during seminary, where he writes that he is keeping the journal "so as not to lose any part of myself."[1] It is from here that I take the title for my essay. I resonate with the fear of losing to your priesthood some aspect of your priesthood. As a priest, I strive to be pious yet personable, humble yet outgoing, alone with God yet present with the suffering and joy of others, prayerful yet prophetic in voice, traditional yet not trapped in tradition, innovative yet not an innovator, a product of our culture while not narrowly defined by it, compassionate yet courageous in proclaiming God's commandments, dispassionate yet wonder-filled. All of these aspects of myself, no matter how contradictory, exist within me and are a part of my priesthood—sure, some are still long on fruition, but germinating by grace.

I always thought of myself as an extroverted idea guy who was more comfortable on stage with a big crowd and a guitar rather than leading a small group in theological study or getting too deeply one-on-one with

1. Schmemann, *Journals*, 1.

45

someone. I am the guy who geeks out until two in the morning on my tablet with Nozbe and Evernote open in front of me dreaming up new social entrepreneurial ventures, sketching plans for a homemade standing desk, making lists on how to improve "to do" systems to become more productive and fight procrastination—a constant foe. I find pleasure in the big picture, in complex systems and innovative communications. I get excited about all those "big ideas" and dream about ways the church I knew and loved could leave the church to be the church. I wanted to take the city to drink from the deep well of the desert and find the desert in the city.

My business degree and experience as an audio engineer and artist are as useful as my MDiv and seminary formation in my mission setting, and are even reinterpreted within it. I serve as the pastor in a multicultural inner-city parish that ministers not only to its congregation but to all in need in the nearby Troost Avenue neighborhood we call "Troost Village."[2] Reconciliation Services operates in the same building, providing emergency assistance, self-sufficiency and therapeutic programs, and economic community building services.[3]

Still, in some more official church settings I will hold back, cautiously resisting certain opinions or reserving a plausible solution to a problem. I was once warned that it is unbecoming of the priesthood to be too entrepreneurial, and so I sometimes hold back my natural talents. How does the big-idea, entrepreneur, musician, priest fit in? I muse with other priests who share a professional artistic background that all of the punk pathos and DIY ethos lends itself very well to mission building, where hat racks become censor holders, thrift stores are ecclesial storehouses for brass furnishings, and bulletins are weekly zines of a sort.

Each of us, each local parish, is universal and catholic, complete in Christ—an indigenous eucharistic community gathered in Christ. Each parish, its priest, each Christian can and must be universal and catholic, offering up the world around them specifically *for* the life of the world around them.[4] Each mission must be unique, therefore, to fulfill its mission. The universality and catholicity of the church allows for it to be so. Uniformity is not unity. This truth allows for even a priest like me to be used by Christ

---

2. St. Mary of Egypt Orthodox Church, http://stmaryofegypt.net/.

3. Reconciliation Services, http://www.RS3101.org/.

4. The phrase, "for the life of the world" is a part of the Anaphora from the Liturgy of St. John Chrysostom.

who is "all in all" (1 Cor 15:2). Even my sin, my weaknesses, become color on the palette God uses to paint his living icon.

I know this to be true but I admit to doubting whether I could make it as an Orthodox priest and still be me, whoever that really is in God. Even before seminary I remember thinking perhaps I was too much a square peg trying to fit into a round hole. How could I be an Orthodox priest?

It would have been easier to be the "coffee-house-hanging, well-educated-lay-leader, guy-with-a-job" rather than a priest. I dreamt of starting Orthodox coffee houses and bookstores, art galleries, and homeless shelters, unencumbered from parish responsibilities and the pious expectations of some faithful. But I read St. Mother Maria of Paris, St. John of Kronstadt, Mother Gavrillia, Grand Duchess Elizabeth, St. Basil the Great, St. John Chrysostom, Harriett Tubman, George Washington Carver, Fr. Seraphim Rose, Fr. George Calciu. In the end, it was their creativity, faith-filled innovation, and holy foolishness that gave me courage to pursue ordination and disregard my fears of being trapped in "normal" (or even worse, ethnocentric) parish life.

Fr. Steven was my confessor for most of my three years of seminary and he knew some of my story—my early music days, my excitement in hearing outrageous mission stories, my desire to serve the poor radically, my talkativeness, my ego and pride. I remember clearly the florescent light behind a dingy yellow plastic diffuser, the bumpy popcorn ceiling, the smell of used frying oil and microwaved egg rolls in the small Chinese restaurant in Yonkers, New York, where I met with him to discuss ordination.

Fr. Steven offered me quiet but encouraging words trimmed with sobering experiences and disappointments born by his family as a clergy family. Near the end of our conversation he summed up his advice by saying, "Justin, if you can honestly tell me that you will be content to put all the energy you have for 'big ideas' into one person, only one person in some parish somewhere, if you can tell me with sincerity that you can do that, then I will bless you to petition for ordination." I had to think about that one for a while.

Could I be content? The faces of people I'd met in ministry came flooding out of my heart—the family of eleven living in a rusty yellow Nova station wagon in Reynosa, Mexico; the children with jagged limbs like branches broken in a wind storm praying with intense joy from their wheel chairs in an orphanage in the Dominican Republic; the young mother who walked into the Rescue Mission after she braved the snow carrying her tiny newborn in a tangle of blankets still wearing her hospital bracelet on her ankle. I always wanted to work for larger change to reach many like them, not just one of them. Could I do what Fr. Steven was asking of me?

I wasn't sure I could be content to pour all of that energy, excitement, even obsession for creating and building into one person in some small Orthodox parish somewhere, knowing that all of that time and prayer offered may never inspire anyone or fix anything. I wrestled with the implications of Fr. Steven's question. And even as I told him "yes", I secretly hoped his question would never really be relevant in my daily life; I hoped God would use me in spite of me.

Over time, I realized the value of the question Fr. Steven put before me. I couldn't yet see the expanse of the kingdom in the soul of one person and the arena of the martyrs in the mind of one mentally ill parishioner. My affirmative response to his question has now become a reminder to me, a judgment seat before which I know I must give account of my life. Like a bold line on the gymnasium floor that I am always sprinting back to touch: no matter how far I run from that starting line I always end up sprinting back exhausted before turning around to run off again.

Some in ministry have cautioned me not to be too entrepreneurial—though the poor need jobs and small, urban churches need alternative sources of funding. Others have warned me not to be too interested in modern art and music recording—though the language of our culture is bound up with art and expressions of its meaning. The list could go on and on of what to be or not to be as a priest.

In the end, a priest must look at the people around him and consider who they are and how the gospel translates for them. Parishes, even huge suburban ones, are dwindling. And the glorious, old churches built in once thriving urban hubs, sit lifeless in blighted neighborhoods. The neighborhood church has been replaced with a commuter congregation to the point that folks don't even know the people that live near the church around the block. Suburbs are collapsing in places as young professionals head back to the city. Many people sense something is missing, but still we continue planting missions and administering the parishes in the same way as the decades before, expecting different results.

I cannot offer definitive or proven solutions, but rather questions, tensions that may be fruit-bearing. I do know what has worked for my spiritual father, the priest-monk Alexii, in his thirty years of faithful ministry in Kansas City, Missouri at St. Mary of Egypt with his wife Michaila, of blessed memory.

Soon after he became a priest-monk and started a monastery I was assigned to the mission church he founded with his wife. Some people so loved the parish they thought of it as a pilgrimage site, venerable, almost sacred because of the years of presence and prayer. I was certainly worried I would mess it up. Before he left I asked him what I must do to carry on. He said, "This has always been a place for those on the fringe. Don't worry about being too much a 'normal' parish. Pray the services daily and love the poor." In this I have found great truth. The church is the church when it gathers, prays, and loves the poor with all it's got. This, the gates of hell cannot prevail against, this vision of the local parish.

This missionary vision puts first the essential matters of the faith and subjects all else to the vision of the kingdom given by Christ and the apostles. It makes ample room for buildings to change or be shared with ministries that serve the homeless and poor, funded by grants and social ventures; for priests and laity working together full-time in the church but not necessarily for the church with regard to payroll; for the doors of the narthex to be opened to our neighbors, inviting them to find the wisdom of the desert in the heart of the city. It gives us freedom to be "a little light" (Matt 5:14–16) rather than a big cathedral that perhaps a few might come to know the truth. It allows us to be consistent with the church in its tradition, catholicity, and universality, reestablishing its mission and enlivening historical visions of gospel work pioneered by the saints, who like field doctors brought the medicine chest of the gospel to the wounded.

At this point, I am convinced that my struggle described earlier is not simply a dilemma young priests experience as they become more fully formed in Christ. The institutional reality of the church is vastly different than current reality. The ground has shifted, the curtain has been torn in two, the sun has darkened and many are wondering if the church has given up the ghost. But there is life in death, joy through the cross. The death of institutional forms, methods of stewardship, etc., is not the death of the church. The church is the body of Christ and he has trampled down death by death! As Fr. Schmemann said, "The church is not an institution that administers sacraments but a living Sacrament that has institutions that come and go."[5] Each Christian is called to find new words to share the same unchanging gospel with the world.

The struggle I have felt in being a priest, to fund our ministries, maintain buildings and reach new generations should shape our parish activities,

---

5. Schmemann, *Church, World, Mission*, 75.

mindset, clergy recruiting tactics, and seminary curriculum. The reality is that the government that supported the church of Byzantium no longer exists. So also the North American economic prowess of the 1950s and the Protestant stewardship model that built mega churches no longer exists.

The church is needed now more than ever, not as courthouse and museum, but rather as mercy house, an emergency ward offering true healing for soul and body. We need to find new ways to sustain ministries that rise to meet the immense challenges of our age as St. Basil did when he established the first multi-service center in Caesarea, the Basiliade; as St. John of Kronstadt did when he created his House of Industry; as Mother Maria did in her House of Hospitality on Rue de Lourmel in Paris.

We need leaders who understand and get excited about the possibilities of corporate L3C structures, B-corps, and social entrepreneurial endeavors. We need Orthodox Christian doctors without walls, therapists on the go in the streets, monasteries whose own industry inspires us to think of parishes as "maker villages," and diverse eucharistic communities, places of rigorous prayer, self-sustaining industry, and real love for the poor.

This collection is called "the church has left the building." My reflection here is that of one person, very personal, of my continuing struggle to understand myself not just as a spouse and parent but also as a priest. So I conclude by asking what, if anything, can I learn from this reflection? Is it that diversity of strengths is important in the priesthood? Yes, my own experience and that of classmates and mentors attest to this. Is it that there is room for thinking outside the building, outside the "box" in which the church finds itself? Again, yes, my experience in several different not-for-profit, outreach-oriented organizations witness to this, most notable Reconciliation Services and St. Mary of Egypt parish. Do we sometimes overthink what church is because it is really about loving and serving Christ who is the person in front of you? Yes. More than anything, we need to love one another, without exception and to the end, one person at a time, seeing in them the universality and catholicity of humankind. If we are to be the church in the world, each of us a walking sacrament enlivened with the live coal of Christ's healing inside of us, we need to care for each person we meet and pour all of our energy into the person in front of us. This requires we become, all of us, a fully formed human, without losing any part.

Bibliography

Schmemann, Alexander. *Church, World, Mission.* Crestwood, NY: St Vladmir's Seminary, 1979.

Schmemann, Juliana, ed. *The Journals of Father Alexander Schmemann.* Crestwood, NY: St Vladmir's Seminary, 2000.

6

Church Goes to the Pub

—Abbie Huff

I ARRIVED EARLY AND took a seat at a table in the back. I set up my Meetup sign and ordered a locally-brewed beer. Before long, people began to arrive. I had no idea if anyone was going to show up to this bizarre gathering, a BYOT—Bring Your Own Theology. But here we were. Ten of us gathered in the corner of a bar. We went around and each shared the journey they had travelled thus far. Some had grown up in a church that had once made sense. Others had been rejected or condemned by their community because of their questions, choice of marriage, sexual orientation, or divorce. Some had never been part of a church, but had trusted me enough to show up to have this conversation about faith, spirituality, and how we interpret life. Through faith and anger, crisis and calm, the journey had led them all here, tonight, to sit in a bar with strangers and share something of themselves.

I am both always surprised and never surprised that people would come to an event like that. Surprised, because I am astounded by people's courage, curiosity, and longing to show up and join in a discussion amongst strangers about some of life's deepest struggles. Not surprised, because I have conversations that point to this longing all the time.

I grew up in the church, a progressive American Baptist congregation, where I abandoned my high school Sunday school class to join the adult class with my parents because the brilliant minds and seminary professors in the room stirred up profound questions and roused a spiritual hunger in me. Faith was a living, breathing, thinking thing that was not made for pat answers or clear cut theology; it was a riot of mystery and abundance that could never quite be pinned down.

I was raised by other traditions as well. My grade school through sixth grade was a Quaker school, where every Thursday we gathered for meeting.

The meetinghouse itself hid a trapdoor beneath its floors, a remnant of a time when they hid slaves and smuggled them north through the Underground Railroad. From worship in such a space to the content of our classes and the books that we read, this emphasis on social justice and care for the oppressed was deeply integrated into my life of faith. This school also was a place of quiet for me. I had asthma, which often led to time alone on my breathing machine, which cultivated this habit of reflection in my own life. The school itself also added to this appreciation for the quiet. Even beyond the weekly gatherings of silence in meeting for worship, our playground was built on the broken-down stones of an ancient graveyard and I loved to sit amongst the stones and wonder about the lives of those before me.

The years took me through an all-girls Catholic school for high school, the Episcopal Center in college, and I had Methodist women pastors as mentors. I became a little sister at the Jewish Fraternity, and later attended a Presbyterian seminary and interned at a Reformed church. Although I travelled between these spiritual communities, most of my closest friends and peers were not people of faith. I felt at home amongst the spiritual but not religious, even with my clearly Christian foundation; I often found among the non-religious that there was an openness and a marked lack of judgment towards those who were different.

After college, I worked for several years as a case manager in the AIDS/HIV community, connecting people to resources. It was during my time there I listened to story after story of judgment and condemnation, from families, from friends, from churches. Sitting next to them in their darkness and isolation, I learned what it was to listen, to hear, and to see every person. During that time I encountered people in all different places of faith. Sometimes their contraction of the virus created a crisis of faith, for others it gave them a deeper understanding. Some struggled to survive, some were ready to give up this life, others were angry at their unluckiness, others made their peace. Two of my clients in particular became spiritual teachers as they showed me what it meant to be faithful, forgiving, and joyful, even in the face of suffering.

Because I have walked this line between worlds of believers and non-believers and have lived in this world of non-faith, I find myself at home there. There have been times when the dress code and language and expectations of church life felt binding and restrictive, and I was not sure how to bring my experiences of life into the hard wooden pews of the church. And to me, this is where we as Christians sometimes run into a problem.

I used to work in a church. It was a great church, full of loving and caring people. It was well-run and had a variety of positive programs and ways to engage in church. The only drawback was that to access this welcoming community, you had to be versed in church culture. You had to speak the language. You had to accept and appreciate church culture. I have a deep appreciation for this culture, having been raised by it, but I began to see that for those who did not feel welcome, those who had anger towards the church, or for people for whom this culture felt foreign, there was no access to what we church natives would call "the good news."

Again and again I felt that the church was insisting to those outside of it, "If you could just be like us, do things *our* way, then you would see how much it has to offer!" But the friends I hung out with on my Friday nights, the people I had grown up with who did not attend church, they did not see the value in making the cultural commute to access what the church had to offer. The gospel was so deeply entwined with the trappings of church; it was hard to offer one without insisting on the other. And for many, it just wasn't clear what was so great about church culture.

I was forced to reflect on a disturbing question of call that echoed in my work life: "to whom are you sent?" I began to realize that the people in the church were well supported in their faith life and way of worship. Instead, I began to feel called to walk alongside those who did not speak "church," to people who were not church natives, but who were asking questions—maybe not about *church*, but about meaning and God—and seeking answers about suffering, faith and purpose, and life. My childhood in the northeast, travelling across denominational barriers, having friends who were not Christian (having dated an atheist which taught me that Christians don't have a corner on goodness and morality); all these things began to stir in me a call to leave the security of the church walls.

For someone whose training and education only recommended her for employment "within the church," this prospect terrified me. But this tugging to translate the good news as I had discovered within the church into a language that made sense outside of it pulled me onward. God desires relationship with *all people*, which means that we the church are called to those outside of it.

So, I was called to the Nyack Project in 2013 and moved from Texas to New York to live in a town where I did not know a soul. The job description was essentially to "engage in conversation, meet people, and discern what the Holy Spirit was up to." I believe we need more job descriptions like this.

* the evangelistic model of ... too many churches

It didn't pay much, and was only grant-funded for two years at that point, but it was clear that this was an opportunity to follow the Holy Spirit's urging and step over the threshold: "he has made no distinction between them and us" (Acts 15:9). In an effort to build relationships in the presbytery and to talk about this new ministry outside the walls of the church, I was invited to preach in the pulpits of dozens of local churches. As I began to write the first sermon, using that week's lectionary text, I couldn't help but marvel at how Acts 11:1–18 told the story I wanted to tell. That text became the foundational scripture for my work, and I spoke in church after church about how hard it was for Peter to step beyond the traditions and trappings of his religion when the Holy Spirit asked him. But when he did, the gentile church was born—the very root from which all of our churches grew. How do we give up some of the traditions that seem so integral to *our* faith in order to create welcoming spaces for someone else to encounter God?

For me, it began by simply showing up. A pastor friend said of this work that one of the most important elements is to have a *legitimate* reason to be present (evangelism isn't one). So I began volunteering at the farmers' market. It was my *entre* into the community and my time there helped me build lasting relationships. After that I was invited to serve on the board of a local nonprofit that does meaningful work with low-income families. I took part-time jobs hosting social gatherings for the chamber of commerce and a local magazine, opportunities that allowed me to meet people and have conversations about the nature of my work, which often turned into a space to listen to their faith journey. I took a lot of people I'd met to lunch or coffee, just to get to know them better: simply to build relationship.

At this point it is not exactly a new church development; we do not have a regular worship service, but *we do* have regular faith conversations and dinners drawing from the wide network of relationships I have built. The more I have become involved in the community, the more I have built relationships, and the more I have realized the nature of my position is not what I thought it was. I am a little bit of a missionary—not proselytizing, but living alongside people in a non-Christian community, being present and available as a friend and pastor as the need arises. I am a bit of an exile, working for the good of the city in which I live (Jeremiah 29). I am a bit of a pastor-at-large, being called upon to pray at secular dinner parties, make hospital visits to non-churchgoers, and be a sounding board for difficult questions and life-circumstances. The most important part of my work that I've found is that I don't have an agenda. I don't have pews I'm trying to fill or money I'm trying to raise. I am simply there for the relationship. They know who I am and what I am and they will invite me into their lives as the Spirit moves them, and *as they choose.*

Today, I am still in Nyack. It has been almost three years, and I still have a job. Since its inception I have been able to fundraise three additional years, and will continue to work to make this call possible, or I will see what God calls me to next.

I love what I do. It is the pastoral job I have always wanted. It's not clear that it is sustainable, and working other part-time jobs to make up a full-time salary has been a real financial difficulty. I don't know if this will become a church. I don't think I would ever want a building, having seen the burden it carries and the way it begins to encroach on why we raise money, why we exist, what it means to be the church. But, I'm where the people are. I get to walk alongside amazing, insightful, smart, and curious people are as they seek out meaning in this world. This is the work to which *we are all called,* and it is now more than ever that we need to be reminded of it. We must become translators of the good news. Our churches can provide sanctuary, they can hold community, they can feed the hungry, and they can inspire us, but it is *outside* the church walls that God is already at work, and we are invited to step out and join in.

7

Awe, Joy, Adaptability, and Sausage: Liturgy and Ecclesial Revitalization

—Nicholas Denysenko

"Люди мають забагато ковбаси"
(People have too much sausage)

IN THE MID-1990S, I asked my grandfather, a priest of the Ukrainian Orthodox Church in the USA, why so few people attended church on Sundays. His response to me was, "Люди мають забагато ковбаси" (people have too much sausage). Like his fellow immigrants from Soviet Ukraine, my grandfather was a survivor. He endured unspeakable hardships growing up in Soviet Ukraine, including the notorious Holodomor, a famine orchestrated by Soviet premier Joseph Stalin in his harsh programs of collectivization and dekulakization.

The Slavic immigrants who escaped Nazi bigotry and Soviet totalitarianism took refuge in the West, even though most of them lived in poverty. Engineers, teachers, and artists gladly accepted work assembling parts in factories and cleaning offices. Their reward was priceless: freedom to worship, freedom of discourse, freedom to live. They remembered the days when there was no sausage, and during the course of over-compensating with abundant feasts made of inexpensive food, they explained to us just how fortunate we were (when I asked my grandfather what he ate during the famine, he simply said "you don't want to know"). Attending church was a privilege, and the men and women who cleaned offices and assembled parts during the week returned to their original vocations of teaching and singing in the Ukrainian Orthodox parishes on the weekends. They imparted everything they valued to us on those weekends, fully aware that our distant cousins who lived in the Soviet Union might never have this privilege. We endured six hours of Школа українознавства (Ukrainian School) on Saturdays and on Sundays, and liturgies were sung with the spirit of immigrants who hold on to the privilege of freedom to worship with passion.

Life as a first-generation American born to post-World War II immigrants presented numerous challenges to me, among them navigating the fusion and collision of cultures through school, friendships, and family life. Unlike my grandparents, we had plenty of sausage, and as we became teenagers, church attendance waned: the church began to leave the building. My brother and I blamed the increasing absence of families on the parish's stubborn prioritization of cultivating Ukrainian identity, and critiqued our grandfather for his lack of progressive vision (though the critique was gentle, and almost always directed at an imaginary stubborn Ukrainian priest). In his tenacious way, he insisted that the problem was that the people had become too comfortable. "If they were hungry or if our country was invaded by enemies, the churches would be packed like they were in the days of no sausage," he insisted. He was right, because regardless of denominational identity, ethnicity, and adherence to rigorous orthodoxy, parishioners always have an alternative to Sunday liturgy. Who wouldn't want to stay home with coffee and bagels, a copy of *The Times*, and a slew of NFL games on deck for the day, when life is good? We lamented the disappearance of the people from church and brainstormed strategies to ignite their return in countless conversations in car rides, on the phone, and at table, because *the church has left the building*!

For some reason, I was among those who decided to remain in the church building. After I left my grandfather's parish of Saints Volodymyr and Ol'ha on Victoria in St. Paul, which was in a massive historic building converted into a church, I went to St. George's Ukrainian parish near the University of Minnesota. The beauty of its sacred space did not draw me there, because the building was old and the iconography shoddy. Additionally there were few families or young people in attendance. At the time, I convinced myself that I went there for the choir, as they had a marvelous group of singers under the capable direction of Kira Tsarehradsky, the niece of internationally-renowned Ukrainian composer Kyrylo Stetsenko. Kira was generous, hospitable, and open-minded. She allowed me to conduct the choir every Sunday, and I even led choir rehearsals, an eighteen-year old freshman at the University of Minnesota instructing twenty or so fifty- and sixty-something singers on proper breathing, diction, and dynamics. They challenged me—after rehearsals, my brother openly shared their comments with me ("he doesn't even know the Ukrainian alphabet!"), but I kept going back.

The challenges from parishioners, friends, children, fellow clergy, and bishops have followed me from St. George's, through a four-year tenure as full-time music director at St. Mary's Orthodox Cathedral in Minneapolis; three years of graduate study at St. Vladimir's Seminary; a mission parish in Anoka, Minnesota (where I met my wife); diaconal ordination at Holy Trinity Church in St. Paul; music and diaconal ministries while a doctoral student at St. Nicholas Cathedral in Washington, DC and St. Matthew Church in Columbia, Maryland; and diaconal ministry during my first academic appointment at Holy Virgin Mary Cathedral and St. Innocent parish in Los Angeles. I haven't seen it all, but I have seen severe parish attrition, awful community infighting, failed and successful parish renewals, three church building programs and dedications, biting community gossip, conspiracies to have clergy removed (sometimes initiated by other clergy), and occasional reprimands from the ruling bishop. Sometimes the news is so bad, that one could become depressed, and my wife once told me, "I don't understand why you put up with this." Through it all, God never stopped acting. People received the gift of healing, friendships were forged, and God was always present.

Despite the good and the bad, though, one trend continues as a general rule, with some exceptions: the church continues to leave the building. I still haven't determined why, but I can speak from my experience as a choir director, seminarian, deacon, and now professor specializing in liturgy. While the church is leaving the building, those who have decided to stay in the building are trying to understand why others are leaving. My essay presents two liturgical principles that can contribute to the building up of the life of the contemporary church. While I will draw on my experiences in the Orthodox Church, my aim is to articulate principles that are ecumenically relevant so other Christians might adapt them to their own circumstances. The liturgical principles are awe and wonder, and joy. My objective is to show how these principles can help the church be her best self through the turbulence of contemporary ecclesial attrition and uncertainty.

Liturgical Principle Number One: Awe and Wonder

Saints Volodymyr and Ol'ha Ukrainian Orthodox Church in St. Paul, Minnesota, was the parish I was raised in; it was one of three Ukrainian Orthodox parishes in the Twin Cities metropolitan area. The three communities frequently assembled together for special occasions, especially for a temple feast, the individual parish's annual celebration of the memory of their patron saints. The services were incredibly beautiful, decorated by the skilled voices of immigrant singers (including many semi-professional musicians) and two *protodeacons*.[1] Protodeacon Mykola Bryn was an accomplished composer and choral conductor with a strong tenor voice and high range, though short in stature. Protodeacon Yurij Korsun was his opposite. Korsun was a *basso profundo* who could chant entire litanies on a low F, approximately six feet four inches tall, who prepared for liturgy by swallowing a few raw eggs and bringing his own incense that was suitable for liturgical singing. Bryn and Korsun complemented one another throughout the liturgy with their operatic calls to prayer, acclamations, and in what appeared to be a friendly competition, offering of the traditional "Many Years" to the bishops, civil authorities, and the people at the dismissal. Our makeshift church in St. Paul, with all its deficiencies, had a long acoustical delay, and it seemed that the church trembled when the deacons chanted and the choir responded. Here's the only way I can really describe it: it was *awesome*. The awesome quality of such liturgies contributed something unique to my daily life. Going to church meant witnessing to the offering of something beautiful from this collection of poor people to God, the air filled with the smell of incense, candles alight, icons, the vested clergy and the people. I knew that what was happening at church was different. My normal church experience was much more pedestrian, often boring, the only entertainment being the social alignments and collisions constantly shifting among the altar boys. But our assemblies included enough strong moments where I had a sense that we were somewhere else, and these strong moments of "awesome" permanently remained with me.[2]

---

1. In the Byzantine Rite, the deacon leads the assembly's prayer by chanting dozens of petitions which end with a variety of calls to prayer, such as "Let us pray to the Lord," or "let us ask of the Lord." The *protodeacon* is a high ranking deacon, and bishops have generally favored deacons with gifted musical abilities and strong voices to decorate liturgical services, especially on solemn occasions.

2. On strong moments in the liturgy see Irwin, "A Sacramental World," 198.

"He has the fear of God"

One Sunday morning, my parish was hosting one of these assemblies and I was expected to serve in the altar (as the rector's grandson). I was reluctant to serve on that Sunday, and my parents urged me to explain my hesitance. I offered incoherent bits and pieces which were all about my anticipation of the forthcoming "awesome," and my mother told my father, "he has the fear of God." In retrospect, I believe she was correct. On that particular Sunday, anticipating a strong liturgical moment, manifestations of the awesome, I experienced the fear of God.

In attempting to parse out the meaning of such awesome episodes, one needs to adopt a spirit of dispassion and asceticism. Clearly, the content of this "awesome" was not my creation, was not experienced only by me, and was certainly not about me. My brother also experienced this fear of God, and we frequently discussed it with my grandfather. It's tempting to conclude that the community created this awesome liturgical content. The priests and bishop (when he was present) seemed to have prepared for the liturgy and engaged it with sobriety and diligence. While far from perfect, the choir was occasionally brilliant, and the deacons added this extra touch of liturgical beauty. But did the three parishes produce the "awesome"? Each parish was experiencing attrition for many reasons, the most prominent being their prioritizing retention of cultural identity over evangelization, catechesis, and hospitality. Young people who were not fluent in Ukrainian or not associated with particular youth groups tended to be alienated and easily drifted away from church life. In the eternally present Christian community dynamics of clergy-laity tension, anti-clericalism prevailed, with strong lay voices exercising considerable power over grossly underpaid priests, many of whom lived in or near poverty. Despite these overt warts, when they gathered in assembly to pray and make their deficient offerings to God, something awesome was manifested.

What I and many others noticed at these liturgical assemblies, the "awesome" content we perceived, was God revealing himself to us, coming to us, abiding with us. When we invoked his name as a community, remembered his saving deeds and words, and petitioned him to come to us and address every sorrow, problem, and issue we presented to him, the makeshift space we were using for liturgy became holy ground. God responded to our petition like a parent running to their child's cry. The "awesome" we sensed was an encounter with God we experienced without complete comprehension. The truth is that God responds to our petitions and comes to us every time we petition him, even on Sundays when we are burdened by distractions such as tensions, conflicts, fatigue, and spiritual aridity. We become aware of strong moments at various times which are often inconvenient, not always in the moment during the present course of the liturgy. The strong moments permeate our memories and shape our approach to future liturgical assemblies.

God is the source of awe and wonder in the liturgy, and the strong feelings that can permeate the most dispassionate participant are caused by the brush with God. As for my sense of fear before God, the fear one senses in church is a kind of holy fear, an awe with the addition of the inability to bear too much of God's presence. This kind of holy fear is not to be confused with fear of a God who is angry and desires to punish the sinner who dares to enter the sacred space of the church. The holy fear one senses in the presence of God is due to what Edith Humphrey refers to as God's "enormity."[3] Humphrey unveils the significance of the prophet Isaiah's vision of heavenly worship, the angels singing the thrice-holy hymn and bringing a coal to purify Isaiah, who is both unworthy of beholding God, yet made worthy of participating in God's divine presence.[4] Humphrey explains the relevance of Isaiah's experience to the modern Christian worshipper: "Isaiah's reaction is reported to us for one reason alone: that we might, with him, glorify the One who is seen so far as human eyes are able to bear it."[5]

When God approaches, humanity is unable to completely withstand the approach. God approached Moses at Mount Horeb through the mediation of a burning bush (Exodus 3); Moses' countenance was permanently changed after hearing God speak the divine word (Exod 34:29); Peter, James, and John are unable to bear the divine light at Jesus' transfiguration (Mark 9). In the ancient hymn Paul quotes in his letter to the Philippians, he says that at the name of Jesus, every knee will bend (Phil 2:10), an honorific gesture of worship. The biblical references to encounter with God frequently associate such encounters with the presence of fire, or the sensation of burning. God's presence is manifested by a fire that does not consume the bush at Horeb in Exodus 3, and a fire that consumes Elijah's offering set an on altar that had been drenched with water (1 Kings 18). The scriptural story reveals God as a creator who inspires awe, leading the

---

3. Humphrey, *Grand Entrance*, 21.

4. Ibid., 19–27.

5. Ibid., 21–22.

author of the letter of the Hebrews to define God as a "consuming fire" (Heb 12:29). In churches of the Byzantine rite, it is customary for the celebrant to recite the phrase from Isaiah's vision at the conclusion of the distribution of Holy Communion: "Lo, this has touched thy lips and taken away thine iniquity and cleansed thee of Thy sins."

"Come and See"

If liturgy permits participants to experience awesome and potentially life-changing encounters with God, why is the church leaving the building? On a related note, if the perception of God's presence could not stem ecclesial attrition in the parishes of my childhood, why am I promoting it here? In post-modern Christianity, part of the problem is an overemphasis on what the ministers and people do at the liturgy, which involuntarily obfuscates recognition of divine presence and activity in the assembly. Pastors who explain the meaning of strong liturgical moments during which one senses the approach of God with his entire enormity have a great responsibility. In my experience, my holy fear occasionally caused me to hesitate, but ultimately repeatedly drew me back to church in anticipation of new encounters with God. I feared righteous punishment for my sins, and I often experienced this fear of divine punishment as a child. Some pastors, shaped by particular cultural contexts and theological proclivities, place too much weight on the imminence of divine punishment for our sins. Pastorally communicating the incomprehensible presence of the uncontainable God in the eucharistic meal does not necessarily entail bad news for those who approach the table to partake of the meal. The narrative story we publicly proclaim when we read the Bible from pulpits and *ambos* tells us God's story anew. When we come to church and hear this story, our experience is akin to the Jewish tradition of the *haggadah* at the Passover meal, when the eldest male family member tells the story of God's saving the Hebrew people from their captivity to the Egyptians to everyone at table, especially the children, who are supposed to request the story. Participation means hearing the story and eating the specially prepared foods, an intimate participation that initiates each person into the power of the story, granting them the same kind of promise of salvation of which the story is the source.

A necessary component of this story is *wonder*. Each divine activity, from creation to covenant to salvation, evokes wonder among the witnesses. The canticle of Moses (Exodus 15) is remarkable for the wonder it conveys among the singers and hearers. By his own power with his mighty right hand, God alone defeats the Egyptians, granting liberation and salvation to the Hebrew people. Wonder or amazement is frequently expressed by secondary biblical characters. Abraham and Sarah respond to God's gift of conception with incredulity. The Babylonian King Nebuchadnezzar marvels at the faith of the three young men who are not harmed by their death sentence to the fiery furnace, and the king fears the God they worship (Daniel 3).

The references to expressions of wonder and amazement in the New Testament are abundant. Mary and Joseph wonder about Jesus, who favors honoring God in the synagogue over obeying his earthly parents (Luke 2:48–50). The disciples and crowds consistently express amazement at Jesus' power over demons, his curing of diseases, and his willingness to approach those who for one reason or another are impure (Mark 2:12). The Samaritan woman believes that Jesus is a prophet (John 4:19). The disciples are frequently unable to recognize him, whether he is approaching them at sea, transfigured before their eyes, or in their midst, after his resurrection (Matt 14:26; Luke 24:37). The disciples at Emmaus sensed that their hearts were burning within them, and frequently, those who encounter him respond with a confession of faith, from Peter's confession of Jesus as the Messiah to the ruler's appeal to Jesus to help his unbelief, to Thomas' acclamation, "my Lord and my God!" (John 20:28). God's power infused in the proclamation of his word remains relevant today and still has the capacity to draw people to repent and turn people's lives around.

The task of telling this story in such a way that a sense of wonder is communicated to the hearers and participants belongs to liturgical presiders. God's power is always present in the stories from the lectionary. In the liturgy, ministers serve God by effectively communicating the wonder of God's saving activity present in each local community. The work of consistently communicating the wonder of God's work that has the capacity to burn hearts and inspire acclamations of faith is neither simple nor reducible to one or two tasks. When ministers perform this work diligently with a careful understanding of their respective roles, participants have access to the awe and wonder God inspires. The problem is that too many pastors view the liturgy as their ministry and infuse too much of themselves into the liturgy, especially by monopolizing the assembly's time with words and extra-liturgical activities.

I witnessed an effective pastoral use of wonder when I was a graduate student serving as a deacon at St. Matthew Orthodox Church in Columbia,

Maryland. The parish began worshipping in their new building in February 2007, one year prior to its dedication. On the first Sunday the community gathered to worship there, the homilist preached on the Gospel for the first Sunday of Lent, John 1:35–51. The homilist's theme was consistent: "come and see," referencing Philip's response to Nathanael, who had wondered if anything good could come from Nazareth. The best way for seekers to encounter God is when someone shows them the way: "come and see." The assembly was overwhelmed by a sense of divine presence and love in granting them the privilege of worshipping God in their own beautifully adorned space. The homilist was telling us that the invitation to come and see God's wondrous works is the ministry of the whole church and a staple of the royal priesthood. Were we as the church to share our sacred space with others so that they could see God and behold his wonders, our church would grow. But one can only see the God who inspires awe and wonder if leaders are willing to get out of the way and refrain from monopolizing the encounter.

Authentic Christian liturgy always has the capacity to evoke awe and promote wonder at God's work, our first liturgical principle. Perhaps those who remain in the church are able to recognize God's approach and desire to abide with them and have learned the story that inspires wonder. As for those who have left the building, perhaps they are seeking a place that inspires awe and wonder of God, the source of our own energy. God is always present and eternally active in the liturgical assembly. In our present epoch of sensory overstimulation and the expectation of instantaneous gratification, it is easy for an experience of awe and wonder to be fleeting at best. After all, can one's experiences in a church filled with imperfect people really rival the illusion of an ideal liturgy depicted by YouTube? I argue that it is both possible and preferable to stand in awe and express wonder with others in a physical assembly, engaging each dimension of sensory ritual participation without the mediation of a laptop, tablet, or cell phone, which present limited sensory engagement. The participant's capacity to recognize God's presence and approach is made possible by humble pastoral ministers who allow God to do his job without micromanaging each step and massaging every part of the message.

Liturgical Principle Number Two: Joy

Joy is my second principle, and this one seems self-explanatory: if a church community lacks joy, why wouldn't people leave? In this section, I will provide some examples of my experiences of joy in the thick of ordinary parish life. From 1990–94, I attended the University of Minnesota on the Minneapolis campus. My parents generously financed my education there, and conditions accompanied this familial scholarship: I was to enroll in a program that produced a job. I was accepted into The university's Carlson School of Management and graduated with a Bachelor of Science in business.

Lo and behold, upon graduation, jobs were scarce due to a recession. I was about to sign on to a sales job (selling insurance) when St. Mary's Orthodox Cathedral contacted me to be their choir director.

For an Orthodox parish, St. Mary's was large, and the music director position was full-time. I joined a staff of three full-time priests, led by Archpriest Thaddeus Wojcik, who was the dean. The clergy included myself and the parish's deacons in a core group of leaders. Besides leading choir rehearsals and singing the responses at services, I was a frequent visitor to the local funeral home and accompanied the clergy on pastoral visits to hospitals, nursing homes, and parishioners' homes.

At St. Mary's, I often sensed pure, unadulterated joy emanating from the liturgy. This does not mean that every liturgical gathering was an affective expression of adoration worthy of Egeria's fourth-century diary sensationalizing hagiopolite liturgy. This is impossible for someone who participates in over three hundred liturgical services a year; it is often work, just a job that pays the bills. I'm emphasizing a sense of unadulterated joy because the joy was neither planned nor programmed: it emerged powerfully and spontaneously during the course of liturgy.

On some occasions, one could anticipate outbursts of joy just by paying attention to the liturgical year. In the Ukrainian Orthodox parish of my youth, Pascha was wonderful, but it ended with the Matins and Liturgy of midnight. We did not have afternoon Vespers; we instead joyfully noshed on sausage and other goodies prohibited during the forty days of Lent and Holy Week. At St. Mary's, Paschal Vespers was a big deal: about five hundred people filled the church to capacity on Pascha afternoon, and I dragged my exhausted body to the church to lead the choir in loudly singing the Paschal hymns. Pascha is universally joyful, and St. Mary's was no exception in this regard. Every year, Pascha began with Fr. Ted pounding on the doors of the church and opening them (in mimesis of the opening of Jesus' tomb), crying, "Christ is risen!" I experienced a similar sense of communal joy at vespers—which I did not want to attend—as we sang the prokeimenon "Who is so great a God as our God" and the other paschal hymns. If this sentiment resonates with you, you are in good company; I suspect that millions of Christians expect and hope to experience joy when they attend church on Easter.

An interesting footnote to this sense of Paschal joy is that, were one to carefully examine the quality of liturgical performance, disappointment would result. The choir usually ignored the crucial nuances of dynamic shading and just sang everything *fortissimo*. Deacons' and lectors' voices cracked. Clergy fumbled over the festal texts and appointed euchology. And usually, someone forgot the rubrics and either stood in the wrong place, or took a wrong turn at some point in a procession. The liturgical celebrations were not objectively excellent; they were imperfectly human. But they were memorable because they were infused with paschal joy.

The consistency of paschal joy is what kept me returning to St. Mary's, and something I value to this day. As a presider, Fr. Ted was a master at interpreting and expressing liturgy as God's gift to us. At the conclusion of every liturgy at the end of the announcements—even if the liturgy commemorated a minor feast with only a handful of people in attendance—Fr. Ted said: "Lord, it is good that we are here." This expression first uttered by St. Peter at Jesus' transfiguration captures the spirit of liturgy, no matter how or when it is celebrated. At liturgy, every Christian participant enjoys the privilege of praising God. Every Christian enjoys the privilege of singing the Trisagion or Sanctus, to praise God directly, without the mediation of priests or angels, a doxology of "Holy, Holy, Holy, Lord God of Sabaoth." Every Christian receives God's outpouring gift of divine grace, the life-giving Spirit whose communion enfolds Christians into the life of the Triune God. This gift of the Spirit's fellowship is given to all at every liturgy, whether on Pascha or on a poorly attended Sunday of ordinary time.

From 1994 to 2000 (during part of which I was a seminarian at St. Vladimir's) I often longed for the freedom to stay home from church. I was in church so often during those six years that I feared it was contributing to a growing spiritual aridity, which is cause for spiritual illness. Now, I am grateful for those six years. I participated in every imaginable liturgy: feasts with the church filled to capacity; funerals and baptisms with less than five people; and weekday liturgies, directing choirs composed of six basses and one soprano, with a median age of eighty. I can still hear Fr. Ted's refrain: "Lord, it is good that we are here." His refrain expresses the paschal joy of new life in God's kingdom that underpins every liturgical assembly. The lesson that I learned from this experience is that paschal joy is not a skill one can obtain from a graduate course or workshop, but it is a Spirit-laden gift from God that any Christian can share with others in community. I also contend that this paschal joy can and should underpin every liturgical assembly, and must be communicated by the presiders, because it is this paschal joy that has the capacity to enliven even the most divided and difficult assembly, offering new hope to people every time they experience such joy.

Many of us know the elements that overcome joy and replace it with an environment of unholy fear that requires the strict adherence of rules. Financial scandals, sexual abuse crises, the struggles of pastors with addictions and depression, the deep polarization manifested by the cultural wars, an unstable economy, and the tension between human freedom and the ecclesial tradition of establishing rules to be observed by the entire community have contributed in one way or another to the disappearance of joy in church life. At a recent conference organized by the Ukrainian Orthodox Church in Canada, I presented a paper on forming faithful Christians by observing a new mystagogy. After my presentation, two women approached me and asked for my opinion on how pastors should address the crisis of the church leaving the building. I responded by elaborating the tension between petition and thanksgiving in Christian liturgy. For most of Christian history, communities have focused on petition: asking God to impart blessings that address specific intentions. Petition was often inspired in part by poverty: when communities are in need, they ask for divine assistance.

In the modern North American context of relative affluence, people are able to provide for themselves. In response to the query, "why should people go to church?" I responded, "because they can." Affluent countries with a reasonable amount of religious freedom have the privilege to gather and thank God for providing everything they need. If several centuries of pastoral ministry emphasized petition, perhaps the time has arrived to shift some of the attention to thanksgiving. The most important foundation of thanksgiving is joy. It might be as simple as this: if we realize just how fortunate we are to have the privilege of gathering to worship and praise God, we will ultimately receive the gift of joy by simply engaging the ritual components and narratives that disclose God as the ultimate gift-giver, the divine *philanthropos*. Shaping a pastoral program that emphasizes thanksgiving through a community's ritual structures and narratives will create a renewed opportunity to disclose God as the gift-giver and the primary source of joy to the world.

Conclusion

In this essay, I have reflected on times I sensed God acting through the liturgy. The presence and activity of God presented awe to a young altar boy who hesitated to serve in the altar on a feast day. A wise priest reminded his parishioners that joy is integral to the Christian life and should be received and celebrated with authentic thanksgiving to God for the privilege of gathering to worship him.

I am not in the business of prognostication and am unable to predict the future direction of Christian parishes and congregations in North America. However, it is impossible to ignore the present reality. Christians are challenged by a serious demographic paradigm shift and in many communities, the church has left the building, for many reasons. But the church is not the building, and people who respond to God's invitation to gather and worship him can have an authentic experience of God through the liturgy of their tradition. This liturgy, the privilege of worshipping God and belonging to his divine community, continually forms those who gather into a church, the holy people of God, even when they are confronted by challenges and pushed to their limit. My hope is that no matter what challenges come upon Christians in today's challenging time, that they will follow the lead of St. Peter and proclaim, "Lord, it is good that we are here," no matter where "here" is.

Bibliography

Kevin Irwin. "A Sacramental World—Sacramentality as the Primary Language for Sacraments." *Worship* 76 (2002) 197–211.

Edith Humphrey. *Grand Entrance: Worship on Earth as in Heaven.* Grand Rapids: Brazos, 2011.

8

The Church as Engagement

—*John W. Frazier*

Understanding comes through awareness. Can we, then, approach our experience—our sensations, feelings, and thoughts—quite simply, as if we had never known them before, and, without prejudice, look at what is going on? You may ask, "which experiences, which sensations and feelings, shall we look at?" I will answer, "Which ones *can* you look at?" The answer is that you must look at the ones you have *now*.[1]

AWARENESS IS THE GROUNDWORK, giving structure and illumining everything. As Alan Watts says, we can only really view what is before us, what is *now*. To speak of church in terms of what it was at a given time, or along what lines it may proceed, only distracts us from what the church is now, in the twenty-first century. From where else are we to gain a true, yet honest understanding, other than how our inheritance is viewed at this very moment.

Engaging where we stop

One of the bits of advice I received, even before my ordination, was that I could no longer look to my vocation in the terms by which I had imagined it. Throughout seminary, I was told of priests who had spent their careers splitting their time between the altar and the parish office, with never a need to take up other work. What we all would face upon graduation was a far different set of parish circumstances. The two priests of Saint Gregory's

---

1. Watts, *The Wisdom of Insecurity*, 81.

in Wappingers Falls, New York and another from Charlotte, North Carolina often pulled me aside to clue me in to what lay ahead.

The thought of having spent so much time completing my theological education, only to have to resort to a supplemental occupation was shocking. However, fewer and fewer parishes were able to support a pastor! And so, in addition to a full course load, a thesis which seemed to take a different form every time I sat down to write, and a liturgical schedule that would make any monastic proud, the application essays to various hospital chaplaincies went out.

There is not much I can tell you about the morning of my first day on the job other than the feeling of fatigue already setting in by nine o'clock, having to wake early for the daily commute to Sunset Park, Brooklyn. I arrive a few minutes early, in my clerical shirt with plastic collar tab inserted. My fellow chaplains go through the morning census of what changes have occurred since the previous day, such things as any new admissions to the emergency room, any cardiac or respiratory "codes," or any referrals from the other staff at the hospital. As the one to undergo training in the nuances of Lutheran Medical Center, by default I carry the beeper, which makes me the chaplain first responder to any crisis in the hospital. I silently reason to myself that it would be better to perhaps shadow another in pastoral care for a bit, learn their approach, and how they handle the delicate situations that no longer call for bandages and sutures.

I wish I could tell you how the meeting ended, but as soon as I get it perfectly positioned on my belt and readjust my shirt so that even if I don't feel the part of healthcare professional, I definitely looked it, the beeper vibrates and as I look at the series of numbers "1111" displayed across the screen, I know that I'm now on my way to the Emergency Department. It's a Level 1 trauma, which is about as serious as a situation can get. Often with these calls, the person arriving is unconscious and non-verbal, and much of the work you do as chaplain is with the surrounding family and friends who either arrive with the ambulance, or shortly thereafter. Early in my chaplaincy, I realized that I despised these emergency room calls, not because of lack of concern or care for the patient, but because of how helpless you feel as a chaplain during this time. What those around you desire is seldom what you can immediately provide. The patient's loved ones want information, and all you can do is report what you know to be certain; they want to know what will happen next, and you try to put into compassionate action the uncertainty that everyone from the medical team to the patient him/herself feels. In this moment, I cannot think of anyone else in the hospital apart from the family member that feels more helpless than I do, and that is where our work begins.

When I arrived in the emergency room, the trauma team of medical and surgical residents, under the direct view of their supervisors, were working to revive Michael. As one doctor stepped away to throw away a soiled piece of gauze or retrieve an instrument, another would step into place, picking up where the previous had left off and working in solidarity with those around the middle-aged man who lay on the examination table before them. His shirt has been cut from his chest, and about five medical professionals surround his head, trying desperately to counteract the damage done.

I stand outside the room, the doors of which are still flung open from his arrival. No family or loved ones have appeared, not even the neighbor who initially called for an ambulance; just Michael, some residents, and myself. I've been called to this situation, so I stand present, but out of the way, and begin to mentally assemble what has led up to this moment. I will never know the years that led to this chilly September morning: what caused him to wake up in an apartment bare from having to sell most, if not all, of his furniture; why he could no longer pay his rent and told that he would soon be homeless; and what thoughts were successful in convincing him that it would be best if he were no longer alive.

After a few minutes, what seemed to be not nearly enough, those in the room and surrounding the table began to file out, and uniformly dispense of their latex gloves in the bin by the door. The last one out pulled with him the bed on which Michael lay. A sheet, with the faint lettering of Lutheran Medical Center running its length, had been pulled over the bottom of his body and tucked softly behind his shoulders, revealing only his neck and head. His face had taken an expression of peace as a lightly soiled bandage did well to cover the gunshot wound that was evident above his right ear. The doctor pulling the gurney, most likely recognizing the look of utter bewilderment as to what I am do next, pushed the rail of the bed into my hands, and in an admission that, medically, his work is done, asked me to sit with the patient in case anyone shows up. Even this simple task seems complicated, as every bit of knowledge that had prepared me for moments like this seemed to have vanished; my mind began, in default, to race: *What happens if someone does show up? How long should I stay with him?* and even worse: *What do I do if this guy wakes up?* These are the questions that stay safely isolated in my mind, as I am guided to a nearby area of the Emergency Department, with the only privacy given by a curtain hanging from the ceiling. I pull a chair to the side of Michael's bed, and in the midst of the commotion typical of a busy trauma hospital, it is quiet.

It is in this quiet that a dynamic is revealed that will remain for the remainder of that year-long residency. As I looked at Michael, his bandaged head turned slightly so that his wound is in direct alignment with the ceiling, he looked as though he were sleeping, and the calm on his face is something he probably had not experienced in quite a long time. And so we sat, not because I no longer felt there were words to describe what had happened or could comfort anyone who showed on his behalf, but because they weren't necessary.

This moment would be the introduction to what I would slowly come to realize that year, and would be one of the first lessons of pastoral ministry, one that set into motion a work that, years later, continues. I can't tell you why Michael felt the way he did, what emotional processes he most likely experienced, and what fears drove him to certain actions. I can't tell you what words to use in this situation, that delicate dance of when to speak and stay silent, when to offer a hug or arm around the shoulder. During that year, I became a professional at these things, and I might add, was quite good. What Michael told me that morning in his and my silence is that despite the work to counteract grief and loss, I still had no idea what it felt like to wake up as him on that September morning: to feel the pressing of sadness on your chest where it actually is a struggle to breathe, your stomach churning because your mind is too burdened with just getting through the day, and how on the day you don't feel these things, when it finally feels the water is receding a bit and you can move a bit more freely, it's often merely to make room for the next wave of grief to land squarely on you.

It is in this moment that I said a quick prayer. I prayed for Michael, thankful that God was present, Michael was present, and I had somehow found myself in this place. I prayed in sadness, not at what Michael had done to himself this morning, but at everything that he had gone through and had led to this morning, and that I was now meeting him in his suicide. I prayed for the many times he had been slammed by those waves, inhaling a bit of saltwater while being pushed beneath the surface, only to rise again and cough painfully. I wonder if he knew that he could call out, that there were people walking along the shore who were, at this moment, stronger swimmers who didn't concern themselves with what he had done to let the tide carry him out so far. And I wonder if he did cry out, in his own way and with what little voice he had, and we weren't ready to listen.

When Christ is teaching in Luke 6, two things worth noting take place. First it says that those who were there, from Jerusalem, Judea, and the seacoast, sought to be healed and as they touched him, he felt a power go out from him. Second, he repeats the universal rule by which many religious based their teachings, "Do to others as you would have them do to you" (Luke 6:31). This same teaching is put forth in the Buddhist Udanavarga (5:18), the Hindu Anusasana Parva (CXIII verse 8), and in Judaism's Babylonian Talmud (Shabbat 31a).

But Christ doesn't end there. He makes it a point to say, "But love your enemies, do good, and lend, expecting nothing in return" (Luke 6:35). We are not to approach one another with the expectation of what we will get in return. "Lend, expecting nothing in return . . . just as your Father is merciful" (Luke 6:35–36). "Expect nothing in return"; to do this we must not only let go of any hope of repayment or reward, but we must deny our very self.

This is much more difficult than it sounds, because isn't it our love, and our giving and good actions, that brings a balance to our whole way of being, and to *expect nothing in return* forces us to detach from the things in which we often see ourselves, our identity? We see our reflection in our work, our views, and our ideas. To *expect nothing in return* and to let go of our self means that we work to hear what's really going on, to explore where it is that we begin to close in and cut off, and why we hesitate to go to those places. To let go of our self, we begin to ask internally, *Where am I right now? What happens when I think this way and I continue to hold so firmly to this view? When can I let go of these things I'm holding onto?* I say this because, in my own life, usually something happens during the day that brings my mind to these questions. I find that I can be open and share many details about my life, and then I go no further. I can share in understanding and compassion with another person, and then I begin to stop, no more. I feel an immense happiness from being around others, as if I feed off of their energy, and then I want nothing more than to be alone.

Christ reminds us that a person gives out of a place of faith: a faith that knows that one's actions are in complete alignment with truth. When there is an ingrained knowing that you are working from where you find yourself, to love your enemies, do good, and lend, not expecting anything in return, that is it. Suddenly an unrealized weight is lifted from our bodies, and we find that we are now, as Buddhist teacher Sky Dawson reminds, "frictionless to the cycle of suffering that surrounds us."[2] Perhaps this is where it begins; we are called not simply to be good people doing good things, but to live the gospel commands without putting ourselves in the center of it all. When Christ tells us to do these things, and to do so expecting nothing in return, he stands at the precipice of truth, encouraging us to leave the baggage of our self, that which we put up to distance ourselves from one another and whatever we hope to gain from one another, and he asks, *how far in are you willing to go?*

This learning to be attentive is what would be initiated at Lutheran Medical Center. I sat there with Michael, waiting for anyone who might know him to arrive. I had been ordained just a few months earlier, and already it seemed that it would be an experience characterized by working through an ever-present feeling of helplessness. I had been trained to have a wealth of theological knowledge. But every experience I had and would continue to have for the duration of this residency left me with the feeling that there was something more that I should be doing. I often found myself oddly silent, not because I didn't know what to say next, but because it wasn't needed. Nothing I could do would ease or fix the grief or pain present in the moment. I saw very quickly where I stopped, where I closed in, and how not being able to fix or smooth over the situation revealed so much of what I thought I should be as a pastor, and ultimately what I expected the church to be.

If this work at Lutheran Medical Center revealed anything, it is that the church was not where I expected. I don't know every detail that led up to that morning with Michael lying peacefully on the bed, as the medical staff worked diligently to put their skills to work, ultimately not being able to revive him, and then the two of us waiting behind a thin curtain in the midst of the emergency department in silence. Perhaps that is one of the places where the church has found herself: in the silence of knowing that nothing else can be done. In some macabre yet enlightening way, the church was present but not felt as Michael helplessly decided to take his life, the church was present when the doctors and nurses knew that their expertise would no longer bring him back, and the church was present when I felt I no longer had the words to satisfy the situation.

The church continues to be present in these absences, in the helplessness felt so differently by each of us. It is present in how we experience one another. It is present not only in what we are able to give to one another, but

2. Dawson, "Generosity."

also when we stop giving. It is present in the withholding, when we feel as though our situation is without hope, when our knowledge of what to do is no longer effective, and when we are present afterward, feeling as though we have come too late. The church is present in what we offer, but also in the recognition of what we are unable to give at the moment. It is noting where we stop and draw in, how we are being shaped and changed in this experience, and being ready to experience this engagement. The church is there, it always has been, our work is simply to be present to it.

Conclusion

> God can be known to us in the same way that a man can see an endless ocean while standing at the shore at night and holding only a dimly lit candle. Do you think he can see much? In fact, very little, almost nothing. Even so, he can see the water very well. He knows there is a vast ocean before him, the limits of which he cannot perceive. The same is true of our knowledge of God.[3]

The church is the one that is before us, where the Spirit breathes and blows where it pleases. We have trouble recognizing that the Spirit of God continues to make itself known in the most unexpected ways. Rather than opening ourselves to a new and ongoing revelation, we have chosen instead to remain in the past, to isolate ourselves from what is new and challenging and fearful. We have preferred to withdraw in fear and close our ears to what the Spirit is saying to the churches.

Perhaps the church has left the building, because they are *our* buildings. Perhaps the Lord wants us to see the limits of what we have sought to construct—"Unless the Lord builds the house, those who build it labor in vain. Unless the Lord guards the city, the guard keeps watch in vain" (Ps 127:1). The church has left the building, yes, but it has in no way ceased to exist. In fact, the opposite has occurred. It exists wherever we stop. I have had a glimpse of the church, this community that extends beyond the persons found within it, an enveloping glimpse made by standing aside from what I thought I knew. Only then was I able to see where the church has been all along. As St. Symeon said, I stand on the shore holding my candle, and only a tiny portion of the ocean is illumined. That visible bit

---

3. St. Symeon the New Theologian, Oration 61, in Ouspensky, *Theology of the Icon*, 33.

is what is being revealed for right now. Thus may we come to engage this church, this *breath of God*, wherever it leads, wherever the Spirit blows. As his body, Christ will be revealed in us as we seek to encounter him here, in this present moment.

Bibliography

Ouspensky, Leonid. *Theology of the Icon*, Vol. 1. Crestwood, NY: St. Vladimir's Seminary, 1992.
Sky, Dawson. "Generosity." http://www.dharmaseed.org/teacher/199/talk/14334/.
Watts, Alan. *The Wisdom of Insecurity*. New York: Vintage, 1968.

9

Paying My Dues

—*Sarah Hinlicky Wilson*

IT WAS AN INNOCUOUS brick building that lay right at the center of a decrepit urban miracle mile of churches. A block in one direction you'd find the Ukrainian Orthodox church, in two more blocks, a parish of the Orthodox Church of America; in the opposite direction, it was two blocks to the great big Slovak Byzantine Catholic church and two more to the positively monumental Polish Roman Catholic church. A short block to the left or right would take you to the Hungarian Reformed church and the German Lutheran church, plus storefront Pentecostals who were the only ones reflecting the present Black-Latino-Korean reality of the neighborhood and not its Eastern European past. At the heart of it all was my Slovak Lutheran parish, a dinky little affair without architectural distinction. Like the others in the neighborhood, my church hadn't left that particular building, hadn't given in to white flight, sheerly on account of financial impossibility.

I turned up in this otherwise unlikely place, an almost PhD-ed pastor to a solid working class congregation, because I was Slovak too, kind of—or at least as much as they were. My father's line is Slovak, his father had been a pastor to a Slovak Lutheran congregation in the mid-twentieth century, and I'd spent enough time in the old country to learn to chatter in the language. I didn't know anything about urban renewal, inner-city ministry, or cross-cultural community building, and as a sheltered pk I had only the faintest and most misleading perception of the importance of class differences. My bishop warned me, but I didn't listen; I had studied theology and that was all I needed to do the job. The congregation took me on because there was no other option available and, after all, it didn't hurt that I was one of the tribe.

The Slovak specificities of the place hung on in odd ways. Everyone spoke English now, but worship on the first Sunday of the month was supposed to include a Slovak hymn. When the organist and I decided to let it quietly drop away, not a word of protest was raised.

It was, strangely and unfortunately, the money that kept the tightest link to history. In some distorted echo of European state-church taxes, members of my parish were expected to pay "dues." The treasurer sent them annual bills and threatened removal from the roll if they didn't cough up. With a threat like that, you'd think the dues would've represented an ethos of sacrificial giving. The reality was that they amounted to a paltry $120 a year, and with barely fifty-five members on the roll the situation was unsustainable. Or so I thought. Never underestimate the grim determination of Slovak peasants, even if removed several generations to the New World. More on that later.

I'd felt a contented and, I realized later, wholly unwarranted proprietary affection for the church when I first arrived there. This little church, just about to hit its hundredth anniversary, was to be my stake in the kingdom of God. I was more than happy to be paid less than half of a half-time salary for half-time work because I was answering the call I'd heard almost a decade earlier: finally paying my vows—if not my dues—to the Lord in the presence of all his people (Ps 116:14). During my first week, I went in alone and walked the place over, just to get a feel for it. I peeked in the dusty closets at dry-rotting Sunday School projects, studied the fading black-and-white photos of ghosts of confirmation classes past, read the various apocalyptic warnings about improper flushing or stove-lighting or garbage-disposal-ing, rooted through the accumulation of vaguely edible substances among the Communion ware (Manischewitz grape wine? really? where was the port?).

The only real puzzler was one of the many varieties of offering envelopes stuffed in the pockets of the pews: they were stamped with the label "Communion Offering." They had an outdated font and the white of the paper was fading to yellow. I assumed them to be irrelevant—left behind out of that general refusal to take responsibility for throwing out crap that characterizes parish life to such a universal extent that it should be considered a mark of the church—so I collected them all and dumped them in the garbage. I think now that was my first act of aggression toward the congregation. The irony was how richly deserved it was, even though I didn't know it at the time.

When illumination finally came, it proved to be another case of Slovak cultural hangover. At my first council meeting we were reviewing the finances and I asked, with no small amount of confusion, why we had an entry for $18 in *income* listed under the rubric "Communion." (Not that *expenses* would have made any more sense: you can't spend anywhere near $18 for a bottle of Manischewitz grape wine.) The treasurer gave me the first of many what-do-they-teach-you-in-seminary-these-days looks and said, "It's the Communion Offering. You have to pay a dollar every time you take Communion." I gaped and floundered for speech. The church president quickly added, "You don't have to. But you're supposed to." I'd heard of cheap grace, but this was ridiculous. The body and blood of Christ, only a dollar a pop! Turns out, back in the old country, when the Lord's Supper was a quarterly festival and state taxes paid for the church, the sacrament was an occasion to place an extra gift for special projects in a little coffer at the back of the altar. The Communion Offering envelopes had a purpose after all. It's not hard to guess why there was resistance when, some time later, I proposed having Communion more than once a month.

For a good long while—say, about a year or more—I thought we could make good on the Slovak heritage and use it as a springboard to new life in the parish. New life was badly needed, since the *youngest* active members were in their late sixties; most of them were in their seventies and eighties, and the membership of the church council hadn't changed in fourteen years (which also happened to be illegal in our state). According to the statistics, there were more than 300,000 recent Slovak immigrants to the mid-Atlantic. If only 1 percent had the slightest interest in church, if even 0.1 percent had the slightest interest, it would mean a dramatic leap forward for the congregation. Our organist was a Slovak immigrant herself, with obvious but undeveloped spiritual gifts waiting to flower. The bishop liked the idea, and I thought it was the only demographic that might realistically find a home here—clearly enough, there was no room for the new locals. Maybe it was a mistake to play ball even to that extent with the church's hostility to the neighborhood; I don't know. It doesn't matter anyway, because it didn't work.

Some of that was down to me. I am a product of intact Christendom, a child of a happy and healthy historic church congregation that tacitly assumed that the culture would evangelize and the church would simply be there waiting when the straying sheep were ready to come home. The idea that you would actually go out and find people who knew nothing about

Jesus Christ at all, and then you would tell them about him, and then they'd want to know more, had never even crossed my mind. I'd known what church everybody in my school went to (these were the kinds of things a pastor's daughter made a point of finding out) and those who didn't belong anywhere were obviously just being stubborn. Fast forward to my maiden voyage as a pastor: about the same time I was throwing away the Communion Offering envelopes, I was saying to myself with gusto, "Well! Now that I'm a pastor, it's time to start evangelizing!" The crushing realization was not slow to follow. Wait, why is this starting *now*? Why did I never think I should be doing this *before*? *And how on earth do I go about it?*

It embarrasses me to think about my first attempt at evangelization. I'd infiltrated the Slovak Farmer's Club, another archaic institution now somewhat rejuvenated as a meeting place for recent immigrants. I had business cards printed up and in my pocket; I prepared to work the crowd. And then I found myself stymied. Paralyzed, silenced, and self-conscious. After an hour of agonizing, I managed to strike up a conversation with a lovely couple. When I finally got around to saying that I was a pastor and they were welcome at church, I knew right then that I had done something not just socially awkward but *wrong*. I was hiding a mission under the cover of general friendliness, taking advantage of their openness to me as a human being to promote my cause. They took the card, but I knew I'd never see them again.

I got marginally better at it over time. I learned that outreach has to flow out of your humanity instead of your humanity serving as the minnow in a bait-and-switch. But, in yet another of the almost endless ironies of this ministry, I found that the better I got at evangelism, the less I wanted to invite people to my church. I couldn't invite them just for me; they had to come for the whole community, which would theoretically persist after I was gone. And gradually it became clear that my church was not a place where faith would flourish, especially if it were a new faith, a fragile faith, or a recovering faith. I feared that if I brought a bruised reed into that place, it would get crushed and never recover.

Even the few resilient faithful who found their way into our church during my short tenure had a hard time of it. One woman, let's call her Anne Marie, of a youthful age (about fifty), had started coming regularly and wanted to be involved. Since I had, despite all the grumbling, managed to up our Communion by then to twice a month plus festivals, I'd asked her to serve on the altar guild—in our setting, a fairly minimalistic task, but one of the few ways in which the laity had some material role to play in worship. The usual church ladies had protested the extra work anyway. On Anne Marie's first assigned Sunday, I arrived at church an hour before the service and noted that one of the old faithful, whom I'll call Olga, was already there. This did not bode well. I came into the sanctuary and found the altar already set. I stalked down the obvious offender and demanded, "Olga, why did you set up for Communion?"

"So?" she said with a simper, not even a meaningful response to my question.

"But today is Anne Marie's day to do it."

"So?"

"She's new and volunteered to do it. We should be encouraging her."

"So?"

So, I was just about ready to slap her smug little face. It couldn't be clearer that, after her initial refusal to do an extra Sunday of altar guild, Olga was not about to lose her monopoly to a newcomer. She had also been the most vocal opponent of the proposed ministry to new Slovak immigrants: "They'll take over just like they did at the club," she complained, and that one sentence told me everything that I needed to know about the real feelings of the church. Of course they said they wanted to grow. Every congregation says that. But many of them don't, not really. Church is one of the few places where insignificant and downtrodden people have any power, and understandably enough they don't want to give it up. Without constant, persistent, relentless reminders that the church is not a club but the fellowship of Christ, without stripping down and away every single practice that allows church members to infer that the congregation exists for itself and not for the lost sheep, it will become a club. With dues.

The apex of the club ecclesiology struck one December eve at a council meeting. Olga and another council member, herself merely middle-aged but rarely in worship and only on the council to please her family, confronted me about the illicit practice I had started of Wednesday evening prayer. The first offense was that I had just started doing it without asking the council's permission. The second was that, while it wasn't so bad at first since it had been summer and thus warm, by now it was winter and therefore required payment for a whole hour of heating. And the third was that the heating was being enjoyed by persons of uncertain provenance: none of the council members were attending, so who, exactly, were these people praying in our church and enjoying our heat? Were they members? *Were they paying their dues?*

I refused to answer. They pushed me, prodded me, and finally because of a momentary slip of vigilance on my part (caused, let us say, by shock at being reprimanded for praying in church) weaseled it out of me that at least *some* of the Wednesday night pray-ers were non-members. Then I was told outright: "You have to stop."

By this point—about a year and a half into my ministry—I was so fed up with the sheer ludicrousness of the battles I was facing and so disgusted at my own craven ways of keeping the peace that I'd had it. The social veneer of niceness that suffocates so much ministry cracked and I replied, "I am not going to stop. I am going to continue to do evening prayer. And if you don't think that's what I as your pastor should be doing, then we have a serious problem on our hands." This led to another long, fruitless, painful conversation that bore not the slightest resemblance to what I thought the Christian ministry was supposed to be. I was defensive and angry; they were suspicious and cheap. Stalemate.

Then somehow, miraculously, the real heart of the issue surfaced through the furious haze in my mind: Jesus. Oh yeah! *Him!* Without talking about Christ, I wasn't being any more Christian than the rest of them. I cut through the nattering: "Jesus said, 'My father's house is a house of prayer.' That's what our church exists for—so people can pray."

The name of the Savior descended like a cloudburst in a parched desert. The Pentecostals were right, there is power in the Name! Everything stopped. The atmosphere changed. It seemed to cool off. One person finally said, "Pastor is right—we act like church is for socializing, but it is not. It is first of all for prayer."

Then the church president began, "If only *one* person comes to pray on Wednesday nights—"

One of the instigators of the conversation jumped in with, "That's right, if only one person comes, they shouldn't be allowed to do the prayers."

The president silenced her with a look and continued, "If only one person comes, our church should still be open, so that one person can pray."

I think that was the Holy Spirit's greatest victory during my whole time there.

I'd like to relate a happy ending to this story. I'd like to say that I had the fortitude and patience to form a new church culture that was really a *church* culture and not a club culture. I'd like to say that the gospel melted the hearts of stone and replaced them with hearts of flesh. I got hopeful for a while when the congregation agreed to let a Black Pentecostal congregation rent the building on Sunday afternoons, but our lack of warm hospitality—expressed, among other ways, by hysterical objection to the number of paper towels they used—finally drove them to look elsewhere. I got hopeful that our parking lot, one of the few open spaces in the neighborhood, could sprout a basketball hoop and create a welcoming space for local kids. Instead, one church window broken by a football and costing about $25 to replace led to a plan to surround the lot with a tall fence topped with razor wire and an electronically operated gate for an estimated ten thousand dollars. I got hopeful that the youth might be allowed to take a role in building upkeep and that some of the disaffected middle-aged children of the old faithful would step up to take office on the church council, but quietly and effectively every one of these plans was quashed. Anything that happened due to spiritual quickening was unacceptable; only those things that lined up with the club ecclesiology or, as a second best, filial piety were allowed to stand.

In the end, it was the money that drove the last shred of capital-C Church out of that building. As long as they were still hanging on by a thread, they could see the point of mission—*somebody* was going to have to help them pay the bills, after all. But after a long legal dispute, a bequest came through to the tune of $350,000. While the cash was being held in escrow, the church's lawyer had invested it so wisely that the actual receipt came to a cool half-million. "Now we can stay open forever!" they rejoiced, as if it were dollar bills and not human beings that opened the doors, sang the hymns, and listened to the word every Sunday. Within a week of the balance clearing the account, $150,000 of it was placed in a fund to pay for the cemetery. As one member put it, "Why are you always talking about spending money on mission, Pastor? We need to be taking care of the cemetery. It's the people in the ground—they're the ones who count." I'd never understood before why Jesus said to "leave the dead to bury their own dead" (Matt 8:22). I used to think it was rather heartless of him. Now I see that he was trying to let the living live: no more paying debts or dues to the dead. In the end the congregation refused to use their abundant resources to pay for a real pastoral ministry, the reason being "we have to save money for our future." A future in the ground.

They were not a uniquely awful set of people in that church. They were not more advanced sinners or more hardened unbelievers than you'd find anywhere; I have certainly heard tales of congregations far more horrifying than my own. My friends and colleagues used to try to comfort me, saying that there were other much healthier churches out there that I could move on to someday. But that was just what was so chilling about the whole experience. Underneath the absurd disputes and misguided priorities, there was a deep continuity between my sick church and the churches I'd always thought were healthy. It was only a matter of time until the healthy ones decayed into the sickness I was experiencing. But what was it? What was the common faulty way that they had been taught to be Christians, what was the implicit distorted ecclesiology or gospel that was spreading like a cancer not only in my own ex-immigrant Lutheran congregation but was clearly metastasizing throughout American Christianity?

I can't pretend I've figured it all out. I have my suspicions, of course. Among others, I wonder how much the church building itself has become the snare to faith, such that in order to continue to be the church at all, the church really does have to leave the building. The proprietary impulse and the money it takes to sustain it do not sit altogether well with the stories of an itinerant Savior who prophesied the destruction of the temple. If the church must have a building, would that it were like Jesus' house in Mark 2 where, instead of reprimanding the faithful friends for busting through his ceiling, Jesus gladly healed the paralytic in response to their faith. Would that our churches' ceilings and walls were broken down by a stampede of needy and suffering people demanding access to the Lord.

I had thought that studying theology would be enough to make a pastor of me. In hindsight, it's pretty clear that some other diagnostic and therapeutic tools would have done me a world of good. But perhaps the most painful irony of all was that, if I'd really taken the theology I'd studied at its word, I wouldn't have been left so helpless, hopeless, and dumbfounded by the experience. It's not as though the gospel met with universal accord, after all. I'd read that in the Bible many times! Both Testaments record the bitter experiences of the shepherds sent out as sheep among the wolves—one of those gospel reversals that gets less air time than the others. In theological books I read with relish of human resistance to the word, of prophetic alienation, of the cross as the world's furious response to God's in-breaking, self-giving, judging-and-yet–being–judged-in-our-place righteousness. But in the parish I assumed it would be smooth sailing. I assumed the church would be full of Christians. I assumed I would be a Christian with the same ease.

I made it a year and three-quarters before I stalled out and resigned, too beaten-up spiritually to go on any longer. It was a relief to leave. But though I experienced it at the time as an evil, I know now that God intended it for my good. In my grief I rediscovered the Scriptures as food for my soul and not just a professional resource for preaching. My eyes were opened to the questions and conclusions of mission theology, which I had always otherwise ignored. I was launched on an ecumenical vocation, no longer accepting age-old divisions premised on an outdated model of ecclesiastical competition.

I never thought I'd say it, but I'm glad I paid my dues at the last gasp of Christendom.

10

Church beyond the Walls

—*Robert Morris*

Interweave: Spiritual Education in the Public Space
for Church and Culture at a Crossroads

WHILE STILL IN COLLEGE in the early 1960s, already headed for the ministry, I had a dream which startled me:

> *I found myself in the church of my early Sunday school days, but the church had changed. Instead of the standard pews, old-fashioned box pews with high walls were in place, making it hard to see over the barriers. As a choir performed in the brightly-lit front, I peeked over the pew walls, discovering a dark and almost empty church. Leaving my pew, I went out into the narthex, where I could see, out of the front doors, a vast crowd kneeling reverently out on the lawn, beyond the walls, praying in a dazzling white light.*

Awakening, I puzzled over that dream. I had always loved church, church services, hymns, ritual—the whole fabric of church life. Yet, in the dream, the dazzling light *and the people* were outside the church building. Even when I was ordained, in 1967, to the priesthood of the Episcopal Church I had no inkling of how prophetic that dream was to prove in my life, or how the shape of my emerging ministry would finally take me "beyond the walls" and into an emergent parachurch network of seekers.

Priestly ministry in the parochial form of the church's life was rich and varied. Involvement with teenagers, crafting confirmation curriculum, preaching, teaching, and presiding at worship brought not only personal satisfaction, but challenges to deepen my skills in sharing Christian faith and practice. So-called "mainstream" Christianity was still a robust and important part of the nation's life. Church attendance was still strong where I served, with little awareness of the institutional decline in the liberal denominations that was to come.

And yet I found that, both in interests and activities, the pull of the world beyond the walls was strong. If the Beatles were doing Transcendental Meditation, my youth group wanted to learn to meditate. So I taught them my version of what later came to be called "centering prayer," a simple attentiveness to God anchored by a short breath prayer or contemplative image. Books on personal growth were appearing in the culture, turning up on the coffee tables of members I visited, so I offered a course on how spiritual practice connected with psychological growth. Conferences abounded in the 1970s about the emerging streams of alternative spirituality, that is the spiritual dimensions of physical wellness, nature, the human psyche, and social structure.

The conferences I attended were thronged by counselors, psychologists, nurses, doctors, and a wide variety of people seeking a sense of the sacred, a connection with Spirit. These people included the never-churched, the once-churched, and the anti-church, but the biggest surprise was that some of them were church members! Many of their congregations were simply not big enough to maintain regular adult spiritual formation classes. In others, religion was about, well, *religion*, doctrine and ritual, not about the spiritual aspects of every facet of life. These people had to go beyond the walls to find what they sought.

My preaching changed. I got more "helpful sermon" comments if I started with what was happening in the media and culture-world of congregants and brought the Gospels to bear on the issues at play. What contribution could the wisdom of the Christian centuries make to the burgeoning cultural interest in spirituality, broadly defined, as well as the social issues of women's rights, racial justice, psychological well-being, and environmental degradation?

Stepping outside the usual parochial boundaries

Having, in some sense, already brought "beyond the walls" into my teaching, it was but a short step to locating the lion's share of my ministry there, though the step took over five years to take. In 1980 I received a clear call in prayer to move beyond parish boundaries into a public educational venture to the wider community. This led to founding an interdisciplinary, ecumenical and interfaith adult learning center "for wellness, spirituality, and the common good," called Interweave. Housed at the parish church, but independent, it reached far beyond the church to people of every faith and none.

With a bit of advertising and a lot of word of mouth, people came. It was as if all those people from my dream who were outside the church kneeling showed up, eager to learn about new approaches to wellness. Churched and unchurched, they seemed to me like those God-fearing gentiles who gathered around the synagogues of the Jewish Diaspora in the first century—the original adopters of the new Christian way. To meet them on their own ground, St. Paul became "all things to all people" (1 Cor 9:22) that he might lead them closer to God.

We offered "attitudes and actions that strengthen wellness, deepen spirituality, and promote the common good." Interweave's offerings stretched from meditation for stress reduction to contemplative prayer, personal growth skills to religious ethics, social justice issues to interfaith dialogue. We developed a network of dozens of local professionals from many disciplines. Over time, we provided trainings in dozens of parishes in the practice of prayer, meditation, mind-body and spiritual healing, and the human experience of God.

The multitude kneeling in light outside the church

The people I met were hungry for God, even if some couldn't use the word; moreover, many of them were drawing closer to God through forms of meditation and spiritual practice they didn't realize were paralleled in Christian tradition. They did not fit the narcissistic stereotype some of my fellow clergy used to dismiss the alternative spirituality crowd, but tended to come from service professions or sought out opportunities for service to others.

They were people like Cathy, the brilliant artificial language researcher, a convinced atheist who had recently begun having profound experiences that could only be called mystical. She wanted to explore the meaning of these awesome encounters with what she called "this spacious mystery."

Peter was an engineer, and church member, for whom conventional religious language just "didn't connect," even though he was a church member, but intellectual passion about the spiritual dimensions of life led him to construct his own theology. What a surprise for him to discover his theology closely matched the metaphysical dimensions of some Renaissance Christian philosophy!

Gloria was a Greek Orthodox church member about to leave church, who reclaimed her faith when she understood how many of its themes and practices paralleled those of other faiths.

In more down-to-earth fashion, hundreds of people found practical help for daily living by being trained in classical meditation and prayer practices. Others found new paths of service in and outside the church opened by workshops in spiritual healing methods, including Therapeutic Touch.

What has always struck me is that they are precisely the sort of folks Jesus was most interested in: folks on the margins of the religious establishment. They are not only *seekers,* but want to find the wellsprings of the holy, the life-giving, in the midst of life.

Growth and service

We found, in the early years, that a large slice of the five hundred or more people who frequented Interweave events were midlife pilgrims looking for new life directions. Wives and mothers entering the empty nest phase of midlife used our workshops and lectures, consciously or unconsciously, for values clarification. A surprising number then went off to get graduate degrees in a service profession, started a career, and returned years later for further training in spiritual practice. A number of professionally successful men came wondering "what do you do after you've already made it financially?" seeking what C. G. Jung saw as the necessary soul work of the second half of life.

Ministry to one another.

When a woman I'll call Lori, a thirty-eight-year-old mother of three came to the center during her third round of chemotherapy for aggressive breast cancer, looking for information about alternative therapies, I cautioned her that she was unlikely to find a simple cure-all. She did try some healing modalities she heard about in workshops, improving her quality of life, but a full remission was not to be had. Six months into her journey at Interweave, she said, "I came for physical healing, but I've discovered that my soul and spirit can actually *grow,* and the journey is now different for me." Members of her spiritual development class rallied around her as her health declined, holding her in supportive prayer at 10 P.M. each night, and going to her house in the final weeks to ease her discomfort with Therapeutic Touch. She adopted Elizabeth Kubler-Ross's approach to dying: a bed in the large family room, surrounded by flowers and good music, in the center of the family life. Neighborhood kids who loved her visited her easily-available sickroom. On the last night of her life, she gently slipped away at 10:02 P.M. during that supportive prayer time. While formally a Roman Catholic, the process of her living-with-dying was schooled by the "alternatives" she found at Interweave—methods that seem to me to revive, in principle, the memory carried by many of our rituals which seldom transmit the down-to-earth spiritual power that gave them birth.

Not leaving church behind

My rooting in, and dedication to, the wisdom of Christianity is deep. I remain an unapologetically official representative of organized religion. I preach and celebrate the Eucharist frequently, and am in most ways a classical Anglican Christian, rooted in the soil of patristic theology. Christ is, for me, the Eternal Word Incarnate, but that Word is also *logos spermatikos,* a seed shining out from many sources beyond the walls of the church.

I put it this way: God has the same relationship to institutional religion as wellness has to organized medicine—a conviction which, I believe, is scripturally grounded. Neither God nor wellness can be confined to either establishment, but religious traditions and medical practices contain wise and vital resources that can aid wellness and deepen spirituality.

I've been privileged to work in a learning environment where the spiritual dimensions of wellness, spirituality, and the common good are explored in an open forum of ideas, albeit set in the context of the wisdom of the great spiritual traditions. Among a population practicing what some call "cafeteria spirituality," we bear witness to the importance of finding and follow the deep wisdom of long-standing spiritual traditions. For me, of course, this meant sharing what I thought important about Christian tradition—but also recognizing, as did Thomas Merton, Bede Griffiths, Thomas Keating, and others, a common human core of spiritual practice in many traditions.

I came to the conclusion that since the apostle Paul rented a lecture hall in Ephesus for a while, a learning community for seekers was actually an apostolic strategy. I've turned my "lecture hall" over to new leadership now, and the new director and a devoted band of Interweavers are testing the viability of our venture in a culture very different from that of the early 1980s.

Learnings

I've become more and more convinced that the church must go "beyond the walls" in a variety of ways, some of which are already happening: Bible studies in local restaurants, "theology and beer" nights at taverns, lectures at book stores, house churches. What about hundreds of Christian-based "open forums" of inquiry about how spiritual practice can renew life? What about a theological approach in which theology becomes a way to see the spiritual depths of every aspect of life instead of staying limited to explanations of doctrinal concepts?

As someone who values community and tradition, I feel apprehensive about the future of a culture rampant with institutional disenchantments and disaffiliations of all kinds. For those who can find them celebrated in lively, prayerful fashion, the authentic, humanizing-and-divinizing images, rites and ceremonies of the Christian Way are taproots into the heart of God and a means of grace, even in this time of cultural transition.

But, as Pope Francis I puts it, the church needs to stop being so self-referential, so enclosed in its own language, forms, and institutions, and go boldly into the world, meeting people around the issues that concern them most. We need to embody ourselves in society in many forms, not just parish and priest; not just preaching, but engaging in deep dialogue with seekers—dialogue without any preconditions.

11

Church over Church

—Mary Breton

I AM ONE OF the lucky ones, and hopefully stories like mine are not rare in our parishes across the country or even across the world. Many of my closest friends are adults and young adults whom I have met through the Orthodox Christian Church. They are the people with whom I share many of my fondest childhood memories. We have laughed together, cried together, prostrated together, fasted together, celebrated together, and prayed together. My peers have shaped much of the person whom I have become, as have the older members of my church family, those who are like another set of parents, aunts and uncles, and grandparents. The church has been the binding factor in all of this merrymaking, not just the local parish. For this to continue for generations to come, we need to find a way to keep the people in the church, even when the church building is not the same.

When I was a child, my father was the priest of our parish in Maynard, Massachusetts. Some of my earliest memories come from times spent at church as a child, and a majority of them are about the interactions I had with the people (and even the building itself). I remember entertaining myself by stepping on the large black ants that made their way across our church's basement floor, which would be renovated in a few years thanks to a major building project that my mother, the matushka (the term used to refer to the wife of a priest in parishes of Eastern European descent), spearheaded. The girls around my age formed a secret club that had passwords and missions. These kept us busy while our parents were in one of those long discussions about the future of the parish that tend to pop up at the end of many parishes' coffee hours. Sometimes when our dad would bring my brother and me along to a weeknight vespers service, there would only be a handful of people present. While the numbers were scarce, often the services were more spiritually fulfilling and mystical than when the whole congregation was present. Being in a mostly dark, icon-adorned church in the evening, with only a few people singing and chanting hymns that generations have prayed, really embodied the phrase in one of our scriptural prayers "where two or three are gathered in my name" (Matt 18:20). At first, the building seemed integral to the experience, as that was where we had all gathered and it had all our icons and incense. But I later found that the people, icons, and incense can be transported almost anywhere and that the deep prayerful environment can be reproduced in a dorm room or classroom or hotel banquet hall. Nontraditional locations to be sure, but, for most of the basic essentials of a service, they fit the bill.

When my brother and I had days off from school, sometimes our dad would bring us to church. While he worked in his office there, we would spend time in the church, sometimes cleaning, sometimes playing. One Sunday, an older man in the parish had showed us how to extinguish a candle by licking his fingers and pinching the wick, so we obviously spent a lot of our alone time after that trying to see how close to burnt we could get. Then, we would wait till the votive candles had melted enough wax and dip our finger tips in the melted wax, creating wax finger caps. For some reason, this was incredibly entertaining. When I went to College Conference at the Antiochian Village one college break, I shared this story about how we would dip our fingers in wax. At least half the room was nodding in remembrance and agreed that this was one of the highlights of our childhood church experiences. These other Orthodox young adults, whom I had never met before, shared the same types of experiences, sometimes the exact same experiences, as I had. There was such a profound sense of recognition because we were tied by these seemingly meaningless experiences. As more people shared their stories, it was incredible how similar our church-focused childhoods had been, regardless of jurisdiction or culture.

My family often returned to Pittsburgh, Pennsylvania for old-calendar Christmas, as my grandfather was a Carpatho-Russian priest there. In my memory, that rectory will always be associated with *holupki* (stuffed cabbage) and lots of hidden passageways, such as the one leading from the rectory basement to the church hall. In its heyday, I hear the massive church hall was filled to the brim with the Eastern European Orthodox immigrants who worked in the steel mills and some of their families. The hall was probably large enough to host two basketball courts, and there were these 20-foot-tall, heavy, red curtains which separated the storage area at the back of the hall from the rest of the room. During our visits, my brother and I would spend hours running in and out of these curtains and hiding in them, singing a song that our mother had sung while playing the same game she had played when she was a child. It is hard to imagine such large thriving Orthodox congregations these days, when the parish I currently attend is barely fifty people, including children. This is one of those towns, as Fr. Michael mentioned in the forward, where the industrial shift has changed the population—many young adults don't associate Pittsburgh with steel anymore, and they certainly wouldn't know the ethnicities that stereotypically worked in those mills. Nor would they recognize that upstate New York was once a hub of shipping and industry.

When we were at Maynard, it really felt like a church family, which made it even harder for us to move to New Jersey. But, halfway through my middle school years, we made the move. Since before my time at the Annunciation Orthodox Church in Brick, New Jersey, a group of kids of various ages thrived. From stories, it seems this is a common thing in our parish's history, as there was a near continuous stream of pregnancies, with certain large clusters. Despite age differences sometimes as large as fifteen years, even the youngest was always treated as an integral member of our little clan. As families moved in and out of the area, there were always a few of us who stayed around to welcome the new kids and indoctrinate the younger ones into our ways.

After most vespers services, when the oldest of us were still in high school and the youngest were still in elementary school, we used to play HORSE and Knockout at the increasingly worn basketball hoop with increasingly deflated basketballs. The group around my age (~ten to seventeen years old at the time) all had sleepovers, almost always on Saturday nights. Sometimes it was just the boys or other times just the girls, but many times it was all of us staying over at the Berger's house, playing board games into the wee hours of the morning until we were too exhausted to think straight. Sundays were our most honored days, and not just because they are God's days. All of the kids could be found scarfing down bagels after liturgy in our rush to get out to our weekly touch football game. Our twelve-to-twenty-person games featured complex strategy and routes, being "Butterfingers!" for the day, and running in heels, formerly white button downs, and torn stockings. Many of us learned to play catch on that field—you learn quickly once you've dropped one or two crucial passes that result in a turnover and your team attempts to mask disappointment.

Things have changed as we've grown older. We still have game nights and sleepovers when we are reunited from college and work, during holiday breaks and the summer. Usually the board games group is all there, whether in person or by Skype. Most of us are able to return for the major holidays and Easter, when we pick up where we left off last. Even as geography and time may keep us apart, I am confident that many years from now we will still be reminiscing on the old memories and we will still be gathering to form new memories, bridging distance with technology. We will share these memories—old and new—with our children. And sharing our children, introducing our children to the friends of our childhood and to the children of these friends—that also will become a cherished memory. Hopefully, our children will have what we had too.

Despite my strong Orthodox foundation, my faith was challenged at college. When faced with the seemingly unlimited options for Saturday night and Sunday morning activities, prioritizing was increasingly important. It was difficult to build a church family where people had not watched me grow up. Additionally, there was not a strong Orthodox campus presence, so I found a majority of my religious experiences in non-Orthodox religious settings. My eyes were opened to a very different kind of prayer from the one I had experienced all my life. We were studying the same Bible (albeit different translations), but the way they prayed was so conversational, as if they intimately knew Jesus as a friend. I learned that it is possible to be both reverent and awed by our all-powerful God, but also to open up as I have to few people in this world, exposing my fears and dreams to our Comforter.

There are also many people in other branches of Christianity who live very Orthodox lives and have found the same core truths that we have always held. At the same time, there was always that question "Is this what Orthodox Christians believe, too?" (Often it was, but sometimes it wasn't.) Luckily, in my junior year a group of about four Orthodox freshmen came to MIT and joined our Orthodox Christian Fellowship (OCF). We were assigned a seminarian, Steve, from Holy Cross, and he was so enthusiastic and helpful when it came to getting our chapter running again. We paired up with the Harvard OCF because both our chapters were on the smaller side, so it was a wonderful fellowship and spiritual experience.

As I have now embarked on a new chapter in my life—the post-grad life—in a location where I knew no one on day one, I am able to reminisce with a new perspective. All these memories are specific to a location, yes, but as I mentioned before, most important are the people and our faith. The address was simply the catalyst for our interactions. Once established in this new location, I came to know, fellowship could occur anywhere and retain the same power. I fear many are loath to consider a more transitional church; or a more diverse, healthier, multiethnic church; or a more community-integrated church because they do not want to leave their building, physically. Because that beautiful (but probably now fading) building was a huge investment tied to that parish's egos and memories, and how could they or their children ever make memories at a new place? First, I ask, how is this a Christian approach? Are we to be like the rich young man who could not get to heaven (Matt 19:16–24) because we won't sacrifice our building for the health of the community? From my tone, obviously my answers are "It's not" and "No." I would guess that there are many, many more people in Orthodox America who have attended multiple parishes in their lifetimes than those that have stayed at one their whole life. So we need to build communities that are willing to be reflective and self-critical and embrace change, acknowledging that they can build memories anywhere, so long as they are together.

We need to find a way to disrupt the status quo—everything from a priest's career options down to the weekly candle order—and innovate solutions that communities will be able to adjust to fit their needs. It sounds like typical engineer talk (did I hit all the hot buzzwords?), but I truly believe that this is a realm that should be modernized with the help of much more time spent in thought and discussion. All this is not to say we should do away with the liturgy or any of the things that make our faith our faith. But it does mean we should do an all-inclusive survey of the church and pull out what is truly essential and what we would love to do if we had all the resources in the world. With compromises in some domains, my guess is that a lot of those resources would reappear. Plus, revitalizing a community seems to have a funny way of encouraging more resources to appear. Puzzle me that.

Flippantness aside, a willingness to compromise and a bold red pen would be two of the strongest tools a parish could wield. Imagine a church that has fifty members. Instead of having a three-story church that holds two hundred people for the occasional large wedding, or the Easter service where in theory every single person listed in the parish registrar actually shows up, they sell the church and move to a newer, one-hundred-person capacity commercial space with a parking lot. The operational costs are immediately lower. If local churches found a space with a commercial kitchen, the church could double as a food pantry or event space during the week. Either option is beneficial, as they are providing community services with the former or have alternative revenue with the latter. Or the same congregation could set up a rotating schedule at people's homes for vespers and rent a space on Sunday mornings and afternoons for worship and fellowship. While neither scenario has the grandeur of high-vaulted ceilings and iconography-adorned walls, these churches would have so much more potential. They enable making an impact in the community with the money saved on externalities and promote living more Christian lives with the collaboration necessitated by the physical opening of people's homes to the church family.

This is my vision of what the church could evolve into over the next decade or so for some parishes, but obviously there are many other models. If people are loath to leave a traditional church building and there are three such beautiful old churches in a small geographic area, consolidating seems the obvious answer. While some Christian faiths may have many schisms because of differences in biblical interpretation and carpet color, the Orthodox often remain separated by ethnic differences and unwillingness to change (both at the local and mother church levels), two issues which boil down to pride and fear. Countless parishes will need to make some disruptive shift in their operational model soon or risk shuttering their doors completely, so now is the time to have these discussions.

I would like to close with this one last thought. Another of my interpretations of "the church has left the building" has been "the church has left the church," meaning people are not living lives that are good reflections of Christianity to the world. While all the friends I talk to about religion have different reasons for either leaving a church or never having been involved, a primary obstacle to their returning is not the church, theologically, but rather the church, locally. Every parish should make it a point to welcome guests, regardless of their ethnicity, current religion, or level of faith while also carrying an open heart and an attitude of forgiveness into their interactions with fellow parishioners and the world around. This does not mean forgetting the teachings of the church for the sake of popularity, but rather approaching each person with love and humility. If we focus on doing this, I have complete faith we will find the right solutions to our problems—all these problems. It may still take time, some tears, frustration, and iteration after iteration. But, returning to Matthew 19:26, when we ask God how salvation is possible, he reminds us "for mortals it is impossible, but for God all things are possible."

12

"Worship on Wheels!"

—Carol Fryer

THE CONGREGATION I SERVE has not had a building of its own for nearly twenty years now. It's a small congregation, only about fifty-three members, most of them older people, but it has a long history. United Lutheran Church is the result of a merger—actually two mergers. Three separate congregations came together over the years. The oldest one of them goes back over 150 years. One was Swedish and one German, both originally worshipping in their respective languages, and the third started as an English-speaking community. Demographics changed and the population of Lutherans in the community diminished. Eventually the three congregations merged, taking the name United, and then later sold their building. There's much more to that story and my older members who lived through it are eager to talk about the difficulties involved in all those changes when they get a chance.

United Lutheran Church was able take refuge in another long-time Lutheran institution in the community. Since 1985 the congregation has held regular worship services on the campus at the Wartburg—a senior living community in Mt. Vernon, New York. The Rev. William Alfred Passavant founded Wartburg in 1866 as an orphanage, "The Wartburg Orphans Farm School." Originally established to care for orphans from the Civil War, Wartburg began also caring for the elderly in the 1890s. At present Wartburg's campus boasts thirty-six acres and numerous buildings where a staff of about seven hundred provides many levels of senior care from independent to long-term nursing care.

The Wartburg Chapel is a gem! It is the spiritual center of the Wartburg campus. The chapel was built in 1904 by the great grandfather of the woman who presently serves as United's church secretary. Its basilica style and rich stained glass windows provide a wonderful and inspiring setting for worship. Sunday-by-Sunday, the United folks gather and those who are able help to transport Wartburg residents in their wheelchairs from the nursing home to the chapel for the morning service. We call this ministry "Worship on Wheels!" We can fit more than fifty wheelchairs in the back of the church where many of the pews have been removed to make room.

I think it is ironic that those who have trouble hearing and seeing are seated in the back, while younger, more able-bodied folks sit in the pews up front. That's why one of my goals is to remove all the pews, put in a new floor with no carpet (we have carpet in the center aisle), and provide chairs so that family members can easily sit next to their loved ones in church. Soon, I hope!

Bringing the nursing home residents over to the chapel for worship involves much more than pushing them over in their wheelchairs and then taking them back for lunch after the service. Many of those folks have some form of dementia and are prone to wander. We can never leave them alone and someone has to keep watch over them all of the time. Others come over in a wheelchair but are perfectly capable of getting up and walking so they need to be watched too. Sometimes a resident needs attention—a drink of water, a trip to the bathroom, they feel sick or begin to cry out in the middle of the sermon. Someone needs to attend to them and the members of United remain vigilant. Communion assistants distribute the sacrament to everyone who cannot come forward and they are very careful to not miss anyone. The nursing home assigns one certified nursing assistant to be there in case someone needs help, but United's members carry a lot of the responsibility. They have a motto: "We're small but mighty!"

So, week-by-week this community gathers for worship. In addition to the nursing home residents in their wheelchairs a number of Wartburg residents from independent and assisted living attend. Some of them walk but many of them come by way of the Wartburg van, which picks them up and delivers them to the chapel. The adult day center registrants also come along with one of the aides who shepherds them. As a result, our average weekly attendance is about eighty, higher when the weather is good.

This ministry to the elders at Wartburg unites the congregation. Members of United are devoted to these folks, and they get to know them and grow fond of them. If one of them isn't able to get to church, a member visits them. When one of them dies, we all grieve, and often members will attend their funerals. At the same time the United congregation remains a distinct group with committees, parish council, women's group, Bible study, and various activities. They contribute to an impressive number of good causes including supporting a missionary who is serving in Africa.

It does my heart good to see the chapel full on a Sunday morning. It is the highlight of my week. We create a large-print full-service bulletin so that everyone can fully participate as much as possible. It's very hard for someone who has suffered a stroke, for example, and lost the use of one arm to handle a bulletin and a heavy hymnal too. Following the rhythm of the liturgical year grounds me and helps me to remain focused on the most important thing—Word of God and the hope of our salvation in Jesus Christ.

I need that grounding because my work involves so many other things. In addition to serving as pastor to United Lutheran Church, I am the Director of Spiritual Care for the Wartburg and also responsible for the organizations' outreach to congregations. Two other chaplains serve on our staff as well as volunteers and interns. Sunday after Sunday we gather for worship and my life revolves around that weekly celebration. The rest of the week finds me busy (like Martha) with many things: meetings, appointments, phone calls, visits with residents, hospital calls, and too much time in front of my computer. But Sunday always comes and we gather together in the presence of the Lord and remember what it's all about!

I never expected to have this kind of ministry. When I was a child I wanted to be a missionary to Africa. That was my first career plan. A retired missionary doctor who used to babysit my older sister and me when we were little was an influence on me. Her name was Dr. Bertha Williams and I remember her being rather large. My older sister remembers her orthopedic shoes. We lived in Denver, Colorado where our dad served as the pastor of Highlands Lutheran Church. Mom was a nurse but she didn't work until after my younger sister was born—ten years after me. My older sister tells me that as a child I talked about being a pastor. We used to play weddings—she would be the bride and I would be the pastor who conducted the ceremony.

We moved to Michigan around 1965. I was in third grade. I was no longer interested in ministry. For one thing, women were not even involved in the leadership of the church, except to teach Sunday school and serve tea and cookies or make dishes for the frequent potluck suppers. It wouldn't be until 1970 that the first woman would be ordained in the Lutheran Church and by that time my interests had gone in other directions. Plus, my father had suffered through terrible times in the two parishes he served in

Michigan. At the age of eighteen I was completely turned off by the church. I remember thinking that I didn't need to be part of the church in order to be a good person. In my experience the church was filled with hypocrites and I wanted nothing to do with it. I went away to college and didn't darken the threshold of a church for about six years, with the exception of a few occasions.

During those six years many changes happened, both for me and for the church. As time progressed I began to feel a desire to return to the church. Every time I attended worship I became overwhelmed emotionally and found myself in tears. I didn't know why this was happening to me, but a wise college professor advised me to pay attention to it—it was important. In the end, I decided to attend seminary, which surprised me more than anybody else! I sort of struck a deal with God. I said, "Ok, I'll do this until you stop me." That was 1981. I was ordained in 1985—now over thirty years ago.

So I went to seminary, even though I hadn't really been involved in the church for about six years! One of the first people I met was the wonderful man who became my husband. We got married only nine months after we met, at the end of my first year of seminary.

Seminary was an exhilarating time for me! We had wonderful professors and made many strong friendships with colleagues that continue to mean a great deal to us today. My husband, Greg, and I believed that church life and home life all fit together and so we knew from the beginning that we wanted to work together. Our first call to ministry came in the fall of 1985. We were called as co-pastors to a small two-point parish in south central Pennsylvania. We were "two for the price of one!" It was a way to get started at a time when people, especially in rural areas, were still not so sure about women being their pastors. There were times in those days when our congregants would introduce us as "the pastor and his wife." But then they would remember and quickly add, "Oh! She's our pastor too!" It was still very new for them and I never took offense. I knew they loved me as their pastor and that is what mattered most.

Our first child was born on New Year's Eve in 1986 and I went on maternity leave. Since then, things were never quite the same in terms of an equally shared ministry between Greg and me. He naturally took on more responsibility for the ministry as I took charge of raising our two sons. When Greg was called to a large New York City congregation, who made it clear that they didn't want a "clergy couple," I went on leave from call. Our sons were young, ages two and four, and I took responsibility for getting them settled in New York City life while Greg concentrated on his congregation.

We always believed that one day we would go back to working together but it seemed God had other plans. Now, about twenty-four years later, I think God's plans worked out well for me. After my three years on leave I was called to serve part-time at another Manhattan congregation where I stayed for thirteen years. By the time I left there to go to United and the Wartburg I had become full time and our boys were high school and college. I had the best of both worlds—I could be a mom and a pastor at the same time. And I had many opportunities to develop my own particular gifts as a pastor and as a spiritual director.

Greg and I still talk about working in ministry together when we leave our present calls. We'll see what God has planned for us! In the meantime, I am being challenged to grow in ways that I had never anticipated. It is very fulfilling to work with an elderly population. I believe that it is a very special and sacred ministry to care for people and their families as the end of their life draws near and they grapple with loss after loss—physical, cognitive, material, and finally life itself. Sometimes it's very hard, especially when you become particularly attached to someone and then you lose them. I have shed many a tear as I have said goodbye to some of the most wonderfully faithful and loving people that I have ever met.

This is where God has led me. Sometimes I wonder why, but very often it feels just right.

13

The Parish in the Twenty-first Century: Community Not Construction

—William C. Mills

Introduction

My family belonged to Holy Resurrection Orthodox Church in Wayne, New Jersey. It is a parish of the Diocese of New York and New Jersey, part of the Orthodox Church in America (OCA). The OCA was formerly the Russian Orthodox Church in North America, the *Metropolia*. It gained autocephaly from the Russian church in 1970, committing itself to serving members from numerous ethnic and church backgrounds. English is now its primary language of worship and administration, and since 1970 has had its own statute or governing document and its own style of church governance, modeled on the reforms of the Moscow Council of 1917–18. The patriarch elected at that council, Tikhon Bellavin, now recognized as a saint, had already implemented many conciliar elements into the life and governance of the Metropolia in North America, including representation of bishops, clergy, and laity at all church councils and in the election of bishops. The OCA is one of just a few Orthodox church bodies worldwide that retain such reformist and conciliar features.

Holy Resurrection began as a small mission community in 1964. The members wanted to have an all-English-language Orthodox Christian parish community. At that time there were mostly Greek- and Russian-language parishes in the area. They first worshiped in various locations in Wayne until they purchased land and built a modest brick A-frame type building which was completed in 1969. Recently Holy Resurrection added a separate building which now serves as a fellowship hall, office space, a lending library, and meeting space for the parish youth. The sanctuary is very simple with white walls and natural-wood exposed ceiling beams and a few dozen icon panels on the walls. Unlike many traditional Russian Orthodox parishes, Holy Resurrection does not have a bell tower or customary gold onion-dome.

My family was quite active in the parish. Mom served as a Sunday school teacher until I graduated high school and Dad attended adult education classes on Sundays. I was an altar boy, sang in the choir, and was active in our parish youth group. I also attended our annual summer diocesan church camp. After graduating from college I entered St. Vladimir's Orthodox Theological Seminary in Crestwood, New York and eventually was ordained to the diaconate and the priesthood, so very clearly, the parish was a powerful formation and factor in my seeking training, ordination, and the vocation of a priest in the church.

Most of the parishes with which I was familiar in my childhood were not too different from Holy Resurrection. Every morning before school I delivered newspapers to local homes and would pass by St. Joseph's Roman Catholic Church in Maplewood, New Jersey. St. Joe's took up the greater part of a city block and included a large sanctuary, fellowship and education hall, rectory complex, and church offices. St. Joe's hosted a parochial school as well. St. Joe's had the feeling of presence and permanence. On the way to school I walked passed St. George Episcopal Church, which was located at a well-traveled intersection in town. Like St. Joes, St. George's also had a fellowship hall, office, and rectory. It was built in the early 1900s and had an air of history and significance. Walking past the parish you felt that it had been here forever.

Both St. Joe's and St. George's are typical of many medium- to large-sized congregations. Many Baptist, Methodist, and Presbyterian parishes in Charlotte, North Carolina (called the "City of Churches") and elsewhere function with the same model: grounds including large sanctuaries, halls, rectories, parking lots, and other structures. These congregations either have large financial endowments or substantial weekly incomes in order to pay for the upkeep, salaries, and regular maintenance and utility bills. Contrary to popular opinion, the average Christian congregation in the United States is about one hundred members or less which means that it is highly unlikely for a smaller congregation to maintain buildings and grounds.

Nativity was established in 1981 and soon thereafter parishioners purchased two and a half acres in a wooded area near the outer boundaries of the city. The original plan was to purchase land, build a fellowship hall which they would use for worship space, raise additional funds, and then, with the parish grown, construct a traditional Orthodox sanctuary. Their original plans never came to fruition. Due to reduced membership size, a series of short-term pastorates, and reduced income, the parish purchased land elsewhere and built a fellowship hall. They never built a traditional Orthodox sanctuary. However, for all the limitations of not looking like a traditional church structure, today Nativity is debt free, a rare situation with most congregations. Large financial debts and big mortgages are very common for parishes that overbuilt believing in the mantra, "build it and they will come." Medium and large congregations will always need space to function. However, in the twenty-first century, with shifting demographic and economic trends, I suggest that newly established Christian missions and parishes begin to think creatively about how they can be faithful to the gospel and foster robust and vibrant community life without encumbering themselves with financial debt.

Twenty-first-century Economic and Geographic Realities

In the not so distant past many parishes hosted bake sales and sales of other home-made food delicacies, raffles, dinner dances, bowling matches, and offered interest-bearing bonds in order to raise funds for building projects as well as regular operation. Holy Resurrection sold bonds and many of the parishioners donated their purchases without wanting their money back. Many missions and churches started out this way and maintained fundraising for themselves only as the normal financial mode for years. However, as Archie Bunker always said, "those were the days" and those days are certainly long gone.

Since 2006 to 2007 the great recession has hung over parishes and severely impacted their lives. Financial experts say that our current situation is a new normal. Corporations, small businesses, colleges, and universities are all reducing staff, budgets, and future projects. State funding for education is being cut. Townships and local community governments are receiving fewer tax dollars due to lower housing prices and marked decrease in new construction starts. The building boom of the nineties has gone bust.

While we will see growth, it will more likely be much smaller. The new normal, as people have called it, also will greatly affect parish life. Some parish communities, particularly those within the Eastern Orthodox family, often need to raise additional funds to re-guild traditional gold domes or replace or fix their bell towers, roofs, repoint brickwork, and replace heating and cooling systems. I know of several such cases. One parish community in Chicago had to raise nearly $300,000 just to re-guild their tarnished onion dome. Another parish had to raise over $50,000 to repair a leaky dome which does not include also re-sealing the windows and re-doing the frescoes that decorated the dome's interior. Another parish in Kenosha, Wisconsin had to repair their crumbling steps at a tune of nearly $10,000, and due to the aging congregation now has to construct a very expensive handicap ramp. Still other parishes spent millions on new copper roofs. This of course is in addition to the regular and routine maintenance, and with an aging, shrinking membership.

Then there are the mortgage issues. Nativity paid off its debt a few years ago. It was a struggle to pay the monthly $800 per month mortgage payment in addition to regular bills. We also had to pay approximately $350 per month for landscaping and $300 for church cleaning which meant that we were paying $1,450 a month for routine maintenance of our physical plant. These are modest charges since our landscape and cleaning companies have not increased their fees in over three years. Thankfully, we do not have to pay additional funds for snow removal since North Carolina has a temperate climate which also helps keep down heating costs. While our income has stabilized, we are never sure what the future may hold. We currently have five months' worth of savings to pay our regular bills. When those funds run out we will have to draw down our savings account.

Despite an uncertain financial situation, the parish has continued to grow, particularly in younger families with children. But all of these details—the ups and downs of membership numbers and less-than-robust member participation, uncertain financial status despite the end of mortgage payments—reflect the deeper demographic changes affecting faith, congregational life, and pastoral ministry in our time. It is not mere secularism or an immoral culture, not disbelief, but the many more complex changes at work in the larger society. And these, in turn, shape life at the level of the local church, the parish.

New Parish Models:
Building Community Not Buildings

In his recent book, *Saints As They Really Are*, Michael Plekon ends with a chapter entitled, "The Church Has Left the Building." What this phrase might mean he has further suggested in an essay in this volume, and all the other contributions are really further personal reflections on such changes in the experience of lay people and pastors. From my perspective the church has indeed left the building. In the chapter he asks several salient questions: Is it still possible to maintain parish life in the twenty-first century but in different forms? Can we sustain the usual or traditional way to planting new parishes, i.e., purchasing a piece of property and building a multi-million dollar building in an era where income is scarce and the inherent social stability of the parish is continually shifting? How can a parish community consciously take out a big mortgage on a property when they are unsure that their parish membership will either be the same or grow in the next few years? Pastors, seminary professors, and denominational lay leaders need to take lessons from our surrounding culture and society as a way to come up with some possible creative solutions to our problems. And the changes and challenges are not only in the reality of "edifice complexes," about the financing and maintenance of church buildings!

A recent report in *The Christian Century* magazine showcased several new mission starts that are trying to create community without getting involved in construction projects. St. Lydia's, a small Lutheran (ELCA) community-oriented non-parish in Brooklyn is one example. St. Lydia's hosts a regular Sunday evening meal and shares in Christian fellowship. While not trying to replicate the early Christian communities, they in fact are sharing faith and fellowship without all the trappings of what one would consider a traditional parish community. They formerly met in space rented from a Zen center. Their pastor works full time in secular employment. St. Lydia's now has space that is available for co-working during the week, perfect for people who need wi-fi and a quiet environment for writing and other tasks. There is no paid staff and they have few overhead costs. Time will tell if these new communities will thrive, but as one seminary professor mentioned, one has to do something, because our current new mission plants are not working.

Another possible new parish model that seems somewhat viable is one created and outlined, though never implemented, for a new type of parish in Asheville, North Carolina by Justin Matthews. Matthews created a model for an urban parish that forgoes the traditional route of a parish and connects the worshipping community with the surrounding culture and community. This is a model that is ideal for an urban or high-density area like a city which has plenty of mixed use buildings and a significant amount of foot traffic.

Asheville, North Carolina is nestled just south of the Blue Ridge Mountains and located approximately two hours west of Charlotte and just east of the Tennessee border. Asheville has an expansive downtown area which includes mixed-use buildings, with stores on the first floor and either apartments or condos on the upper floors. Asheville is a pedestrian city with many restaurants, cafés, bookstores, and boutiques. This modern parish model calls for either a long-term rental or purchase of a community center located in the middle of the Main Street shopping district. The primary space would be used as either a coffee house, used bookstore, or a general meeting place where people would come and make use of the building during the week. There would be space reserved for a traditional Orthodox chapel complete with icons, candle stands, iconostasis, and altar. The chapel would be open for people to come and sit quietly for prayer, to light a candle, or just to "come and see." Regular services would be conducted on the weekends, perhaps Great Vespers on Saturday night or some form of evening prayer and then a regular Divine Liturgy on Sunday morning. During the weekdays the rest of the building would be primarily for other purposes. Depending on the business model, the new parish could host guest speakers and have meeting spaces for local writer's groups, book club meetings, mom's night out, wine tastings, or host poetry readings or local authors, even a performance space for musicians. This new type of parish would literally serve as a crossroads between the church and the world, a place where Orthodox Christians could live, work, and pray, maintaining a steady source of income as well as serving as an Orthodox witness to the local neighborhood. This would also mean that the parish would not have the usual external trappings of an Orthodox building such as expensive hand-painted icons, bell towers, and the typical Russian Orthodox gilded gold onion domes. This new "non-parish" would feel more like a real living and breathing community and would be a self-sustaining enterprise. This new parish model would require much planning and work but would be a creative Christian community.

This model is not totally new. Currently, a pan-Orthodox venture in Colorado Springs called Agia Sophia Coffee House and Bookstore is up and running. While the coffee shop does not have a chapel in it, they do have regular business hours and serve coffee, tea, and sandwiches, and have meeting rooms for ten to fifteen people as well as a full range of Orthodox Christian books and icons for sale. Another similar business is located in Harrisburg, Pennsylvania. All they would need to do would be to create a space in their building for a chapel and they would then have this type of newer Orthodox parish community. Other examples of such alternative communities abound. Carol Howard Merritt drew attention via her blog, "Tribal Church," to one at which her pastor-spouse works, Mercy Junction, Chattanooga, Tennessee.

Other congregations are experimenting in different ways. Some are sharing rented space and others are purchasing property and sharing it with other ecclesial communities. This cuts back on incurring huge financial burdens but also requires a lot of cooperation and goodwill. One local Jewish synagogue in Davidson, North Carolina for example, has used worship space at St. Alban's Episcopal Church. The synagogue met on Saturday mornings and were able to utilize the parish for worship, adult education, and fellowship. Then on Sunday, the space was used by the parish community. Some parish communities are utilizing space hosted by the local YMCA or other local venues. Creativity, not construction, is the name of the game in today's world.

Nativity—An Experiment in Community Building

I arrived at Nativity in June 2000 and was received with a warm welcome by parishioners eager for growth and expansion. Years of financial and personal challenges had sent the parish community into a downward spiral. Upon arrival I learned that I was the seventh priest in nineteen years and the people were ready to move forward. Having a then new, young pastor and new members brought some much needed energy to the congregation. Income and spirits were up. A few parishioners wanted to purchase land near the new I-485 Outer Beltway which encircles Charlotte and its suburbs. The parishioners wanted to build a traditional Orthodox sanctuary, fellowship hall, rectory, and cemetery on eight acres of prime land on a hill overlooking I-485. Very much a "back to the future" move. Architectural renderings were drawn, discussions ensued, and people were excited. However, the steep price tag along with some shifting in financial trends in the community put all of this on the backburner. What to do?

After much discussion, debate, and soul searching our community decided against construction and decided to focus on creating a robust and vibrant community. We realized that Nativity was a wonderful parish community but was susceptible to shifting economic and demographic trends. We also realized that many families remained at Nativity for short periods due to job transfers or other economic reasons. Frequent transitions also meant lower weekly contributions to help support our budget. Therefore, after much discussion and soul searching we decided on building community and not buildings.

The parish leadership understood that while people came to church each week, they really didn't know each other. There were few strong bonds between families. We decided on having two major picnics a year, one in the fall to kick off our church school program and another in the early summer to end it. People brought food and we had games and fellowship. We also hosted a monthly work day where families could come to help out on small parish projects such as weeding, planting, mulching, as well as painting and light carpentry work. We ended the day with lunch and fellowship. These work days fostered stronger family bonds and social cohesion within the community.

However, we also realized that community wasn't just the "parish community" but also included the local community as well. There were no outreach programs when I arrived in the parish. People basically came to church each week and left; there was no connection between the church and the world, the parish and Main Street. People wanted to do something but didn't know what to do. Rather than go out to the local community we decided to bring the community into the parish. I arranged for five local outreach programs to send a volunteer director to attend our Sunday Divine Liturgy, and during our coffee hour they would lead a short presentation about how we could assist their ministry. After hearing about five or six of these inspirational speakers we decided on helping the local men's Rescue Mission. We would cook a hot lunch once per month for one hundred men. Our parish would purchase all of the supplies, cook the meal, and then eat with them. We have been doing this for thirteen years now. After the men's Rescue Mission ministry was going well it was easier to adopt other ministries. Today our small parish of fifty adults hosts eight outreach projects such as donating canned food to the local Loaves and Fishes Food Bank, collecting diapers, wipes, and baby formula for the Florence Crittenden Center, making blankets for the national Project Linus Blanket Program, as well as collecting backpacks and filling them with school supplies for the local school system. Our ministries have not only helped the local community, but have strengthened our parish community as well. Parishioners are now more open to helping and volunteering with these ministries and oftentimes we have many more helpers than we need! Our focus in creating community rather than constructing buildings has really paid off.

It is also very fortunate that we never moved forward with the original building project on that hill overlooking I-485. In 2008, just as the great recession hit, our parish lost about twenty-five parishioners due to work-related relocation and the start of a new Orthodox mission about forty minutes south of our parish. This loss in parishioners also translated into a $25,000 decrease in income. Times were tough and we had to go into survival mode which meant a reduction in salaries as well as in other budgetary expenditures. For three years we passed a bare-bones budget and requested financial assistance from our diocese. The alternative was to draw down our building fund which meant that we'd have no additional savings. If we had built that large sanctuary, hall, and cemetery we wouldn't have been able to pay for the mortgage, let alone our other expenses. Having a smaller property and no debts allowed us to weather the very difficult financial storm that hit. Thankfully, our parish has weathered that storm but it also taught us important financial lessons. More so, it has taught us about what really constitutes a parish—the community of the people of God who pray and gather there.

Conclusion

Christianity has a long and beautiful history of church buildings: the famous cathedrals such as Notre Dame in Paris, York Minster in England, and St. Patrick's in Manhattan. However, the days of building large edifices and incurring a massive debt are way behind us now. It was one thing for pastors to send out pleas for funds when parishioners considered their local parish their spiritual home. After all, they could easily walk to it and hear the bells. Now many parishes are regional, drawing from many townships and counties and school districts. Those days of the village church are long gone. The average family moves more frequently than ever and often has very little connection to the local parish except for Sunday worship. Most young families today wouldn't think twice about spending an entire weekend baking banana bread or purchasing bonds to help pay for the mortgage or repair a bell tower: they simply won't do it. In the twenty-first century pastors and lay leaders would benefit from literally "thinking outside the box" when it comes to starting new Christian communities, focusing their energy and efforts in having new ways for building community, not construction.

14

God Is with Us, God Is the future

—Wongee Joh

Thomas answered him, "My Lord and my God!" Jesus said to him, "Have you believed because you have seen me? Blessed are those who have not seen, yet have come to believe."—John 20:29

YESTERDAY I DID THE memorial service for a son of a faithful member. This is the second child buried by this member. A parent never expects to bury their child, though it is a fear that many parents have. This time, she shared that she was prepared to answer back to anyone who might say, "at least you have your other children." Her first child died in childhood. Her second child, Tom, battled terminal cancer and died at the same age as I am now. During my visits with him at the veteran's hospital where he received hospice care until his death, he shared that he chose not to be confirmed as a youth even though he went through all the classes. I learned through my training in chaplaincy to listen to the stories people share with us. Of all the many stories in their lives, the stories people choose to share have relevance and meaning. This particular story hovered over and with Tom and me, in the many conversations we shared afterwards and the many we did not. I remember in that conversation, how his voice grew angry while telling me about his choice, how he felt the church took from those who were with-out enough for themselves. He did not understand why his mom, a single mother after his parents divorced, gave so much to the church. I remember also the tears that found their way out through the corners of his eyes and how he turned away in silence. It was like he was saying to me, "Take that! It was my choice not to get confirmed and I knew what my choice was even as a teen. Take it or leave it." I remember how in that space of anger, resentment, pain, remembering, and turning away there was a clear statement that there was nothing I could say or should say. Nothing that I sensed and felt needed to be said at all. It was not easy sitting in the silence with his back towards me until the tension subsided from the air and his breathing came to an almost sleepy silence. Sleepy silences are both uncomfortable in their intimacy and a comforting presence: we are not alone with our feelings. I continued to visit Tom and was privileged by grace to trust God's prevenient grace present back in those confirmation classes, here and now, and in Tom's future.

Tom's service was held at the local funeral home. These days I do more services at funeral homes than in the church. The funeral directors often work with families from one generation to the next, while United Methodist pastors seem to come and go through the itinerant system of appointments. Funeral homes have larger parking lots than most churches and provide more comfortable spaces for folks who are not churchgoers. No hard pews in the funeral homes. It's air-conditioned. The services are offered with convenient options for visitors. They can stop in for the wake and leave before the religious service. They have multiple times to choose from to visit with the family. Some come during the day before kids come home from school, some come after their workday. Some stay longer, before and after the services, and some come and stay briefly to offer their respects. Some aren't even noticed as they seem to discreetly and almost anonymously offer their sympathies between the flow of all the comings and goings of visitors.

For me, the services held at funeral homes are different from the services I hold in the church. I do not mean different in any bad/worse or good/better comparative sense. I just mean different. Perhaps they are even more different for the folks who are regular Sunday attendees at worship. I assume that when services are held at the church, irregular Sunday churchgoers or the unchurched also feel that the service is different in the same way. The only folks for whom I have done the services in the church sanctuary itself have been older members; most are older than my parents. I have done a funeral service in a college chapel for a close friend who died while a professor at the school. Other than those exceptions, most services at which I have presided are held at the funeral homes. So, when I do a funeral service in the church, fewer as my years in ministry increase, there is both a certain formality and informality about it, at least for me. I feel a gentle humility within my heart that the "Service of Death and Resurrection," as we call it in the United Methodist tradition, an opportunity to celebrate the life of the deceased, is often in the same space in which they had been baptized, confirmed, married, and baptized their children; where their parents held their services of death and resurrection; where every "Service of Death and Resurrection" has been held for members of their own immediate families and friends. The church is both the physical space and community with whom they have prayed, praised, offered thanksgivings, shouted with joy and cried tears of pain while sharing their stories. It may also have been where silences were louder than any word/Word, where folks were sent out or come home to, where visitors wandered in and found wonder. It could also be the space where rejections and abuses occurred, and difficult choices healed or broke relationships. It is often a space where physical changes to aging buildings require many conversations. They cannot control the changes outside the church, but maybe the changes regarding the building can be managed. The church is not the building, but a physical space that is more than just or merely brick and mortar. Spaces offer us ways to remember, and remembering through the ways worship unfolds in those spaces can be life-giving, especially in times of death.

After the funeral service for Tom, everyone was invited back to the church hall. Interestingly, the reception is usually held at the church. The noisy fans were running in the heat of another humid summer day. The fans muted the different conversations around the tables. In the heat, hugging people is literally a sticky business. The parking lot overflows onto the country road and the townspeople drive around the lines of cars. Even they know this is not a regular Sunday worship. No alcohol is allowed in the fellowship hall, probably the reason why we have more funeral receptions than wedding receptions hosted in the hall.

The tables with refreshments and desserts had been set up by the same faithful, diehard bunch of church folks while the families were at the funeral home for the service. The same desserts we often have at our bi-annual spaghetti dinner fundraiser make quite a spread. The desserts usually draw in the whole town at our spaghetti dinners, where I am always shocked by how many people return for participation and support. I'm told that since there is nothing else happening in our little hamlet, it's the event where everyone comes to catch up. I wish I had the same steady attendance in worship for the last seven years. Maybe my sermons are not dessert-like enough.

The food is served by women and men who understand that death, no matter the circumstances, is not easy. I offer grace, remembering God is present in the breaking of bread together and in our life, even and especially in our experiences of death. We remember we will feast together at the heavenly banquet. We take a look around at each face around this particular table and give thanks for one another. God walks the path with us, we hope.

Although Psalm 23 is a common reading at funeral services, until Tom's funeral I had never offered my message based on this well-known text. It is almost like a national anthem in its familiarity to the churched and unchurched alike. The text usually seems to speak for itself. Tom's service was the first in which I chose to highlight the words from the psalm. Reading words like "leads, restores, comforts, anoints, prepares," and sharing what I read in one of the commentaries on the psalm, I noted that these words are not just words of what the Good Shepherd promises us in this season of grief, but also what is promised during the entirety of our lives, trusting that our relationships with the Good Shepherd are in our future as well.

Reflecting on ministry in the twenty-first century alongside the sense that "the church has left the building," I'm not sure what it is that I can say. Churches are looking for ways to navigate a new terrain. I'm like the lost sheep, and I think maybe the church I serve feels like a lost sheep because of the confusion and fears generated by the evidence of declining membership, the denomination's talk of revitalization, and living in a world where the world seems larger than ever before. In our lost-ness, we tried to do all that we are told makes for a vital congregation. We created a small group ministry and that helped connect new folks within the church, helping them to feel that they belonged in a church whose history included a member's great-grandmother who rode a horse during the revolutionary birth of a new nation. We focused on Sunday school and youth, taking mission trips to the Appalachia area in the south. Now, having completed college, those same young people have jobs and no longer live in this little hamlet. We took the old choir pews near the altar out to make space for our praise team to play contemporary music. We lost a member because we moved those pews from the front of the church to the narthex. This member felt we were changing the church into a garage, and inviting in a rock band. Yet the members of the praise team included the mother and sister of Tom, long-time members of the church. This was not the first time the church went through a season of challenges and changes, and it is not the first time the seasons and challenges outside the church changed. The seasons of change may not be as delineated as we like to think, even as we are called to live spiritual lives counter-cultural to the times we live in. In my short season as pastor in this church, I have grown to trust the Good Shepherd more and more.

I had an experience of being led when recently our little church that has had part-time ministers for its entire 250-year history—a church I've heard folks call the "Laura Ingalls' little church on the prairie"—became part of a larger parish, a cooperative connecting six churches sharing a ministry team into which I transitioned. I trust we are being led just as I was led here as the new pastor.

I recall a conversation I had when I first arrived at this "little church with a big heart." A member approached me regarding changes I was introducing. I was trying to help break the path dependence of the congregation, the insistence that because "we have always done it this way" we should continue to do it this way, and lead them towards trusting a new, even improbable, way—a way that they may not initially desired. I was told clearly by this member that she had been born, baptized, confirmed, and married in this church, that her children who were also born, confirmed, and likely to be married in this church, and that she would be buried in this church by a different pastor long after someone like me had moved on. I was amazed by the privilege that the certainty of her faith and history gave her. My faith probably had a ring of certainty like hers, something we have in common. I reminded her that it is okay; that unlike her, I was born into one church in one country, baptized in another denomination in another country, confirmed in a church in a different state from where I was baptized, married in another, and my children were baptized in another, were likely each to be confirmed in different churches, and, for that matter, it is hardly difficult to imagine this happening in different countries. I wasn't even certain if one day I would be able to marry my children in a denomination in which same-sex marriage was allowed. (Who knew my kids' sexual orientation at this time?) In fact, I wasn't sure where I would be buried and what church was going to bury me. I have no idea when and where I will die. It's a mystery, an unknown to me. It is even possible that she may see me buried in that church herself. I shared the one thing we could be certain of together: that God loves us and our differences are a gift to each other. Maybe both of us were feeling a little lost in the ever-changing present and feeling anxious about the future of our church, and we each had to remember our stories of God's faithfulness. I do know that God was restoring both of us into an image that neither one of us could imagine for ourselves without each other. Since that conversation, we have been present with one another through many funeral services of church members, including her mom and brother. It was humbling for me to officiate at their services and be in the presence of their loved ones. I'm grateful for her prayers and presence as my own uncle, mother, father-in-law, and cousin also died during those same periods. Our relationship is not what it was before we had that conversation and it will not be the same in the future from what it is now. Amazing grace, indeed.

I still serve this church as part of the new larger parish, alongside the other five churches, as one leader within a ministry team of five servant leaders. For the two years previous to the merge I had also been serving one of the other five churches. In fact, at least ten years prior to my arrival, that church was one of the larger churches in the area. It had been considered one the flagship churches in our conference. I was told that the high water mark had been when the worship service had more than 200 folks in the pews and the education wing was added. The education wing is now rented out to a growing private school and our average attendance in the pews each Sunday is below thirty-five. The folks who used to walk to the church located on the main street no longer walked to church. What used to be a typical American main street in town now looks different due to changing demographics and the suburban sprawl beyond the center of town. According to Wikipedia, the town had the highest population of a single immigrant group in the entire nation. The Spanish-speaking congregations that rent our space for their worship use our building more than we do. The building is also shared throughout the year by various community groups and non-profit groups which provide services to meet the needs of the changing population around us. We partner with many of these groups, and our shared space enables mission opportunities through the use of the space. When I arrived as the new pastor, the weather vane on the church building with its high steeple was knocked down during Superstorm Sandy. It sat in broken pieces in my office. There is now a new cross on the steeple, and the weather vane is being restored and will be given to the local historical society. Beautiful stained glass windows adorn the sanctuary on both sides of the pulpit; one is of Jesus as the Good Shepherd holding a sheep in his arms.

One vital ministry at this church is providing shelter for the homeless in its building via an ecumenical weekly rotation throughout the winter. It takes the community working together to ensure that "no person dies on our watch." The program was created after two homeless folks were found frozen to death in the local park one winter. The church fellowship hall is set up with cots and hot meals are prepared every day during the winter months. We received not only more grant money for the shelter, but also a generous donation to install a new heating system. In the winter months, those without shelter can find space that offers food and comfortable warmth through the night. The church folks find some comfort in that, although we cannot change overnight the systems that maintain unjust conditions as the status quo for folks living in poverty; those considered "illegal aliens" (how are humans illegal aliens?); those suffering from addictions, metal illness, and conditions that prevent employment or employment that pays a sustainable living wage. Even though the reality is that there is more to be done, we are in it together through the cold nights of winter. The same God present at our worship in the sanctuary is also present amongst the cots in the fellowship hall.

At the beginning of my ministries I thought the most difficult aspect would be getting through the season of what I like to think of as our winter—trying to awaken folks to live in the present and let go their past memories of "how it use to be," those days when there were two hundred members sitting in the pews, the days when a new education wing was required, or when the church had enough faithful families to run fundraising dinners every month of the year to buy a parsonage. Those days are remembered as part of a wonderful and "God-has-always-been-good-to-us" past. The loss of having sold that parsonage is part of the new present. What I learned in the process of becoming part of the community of these churches is that these memories are necessary. To remember that "God has always been good to us" sustains the communities in the present time as they face the realities of all that is changing and is different. Part of the challenge for the churches—the current reality of declining membership, aging buildings, and changing communities—is how we trust and respond faithfully in ways that bring about the reality that God will always be faithful to us and is in our future. I find myself in ministry feeling a lot like the disciples who came to realize that the reign of God would unfold in ways they had not expected or imagined. In many ways we have an advantage over the disciples as we have their witness to us, and in fact Jesus' own blessings to us, "Blessed are those who have not seen and yet have come to believe" (John 20:29). Death is not the end. Still, when we face what feels like a dying of the church, we wonder what resurrection looks like and what it means. We easily doubt if resurrection was, is, or will be. In the waiting, the doubting, and the wondering, I pray and trust that the Spirit of life will anoint us, as we need that same Spirit that was in Christ and raised Christ from the dead to raise us also into new life (Rom 8:11). It is difficult sometimes to feel the breath of new life. The Spirit anoints even when we are not receptive, maybe even groans on our behalf for such happenings. In both churches that I serve, calling folks to trust that our church has a future, that it is still living into a future, seems to be the most challenging task of ministry today.

Remembering past faithfulness is important, as long as it does not prevent one from facing the fears and realities of our present condition and experiencing God's presence with us even now. Part of the purpose of worship on Sundays is to remind the gathered community of God's faithfulness, that we are experiencing God's presence now, and that we walk into God's future. In remembering as a community, we may be able to face the truth of our present times. The word for truth in Greek is *aletheia*, meaning "what is not forgotten." Remembering may be our way into our future, a future in which surely we can proclaim that God's love and presence is with us, a future in which we remember that our hearts were filled, our cups ran over, and in which we continue to dwell with one another and in God. The future in which the church is present may mean understanding that the dying church is not the end; resurrection and new life in God is promised and has already been given to every present age.

The churches I serve are both dying and living. I've experienced both happening. I'm reminded of Dietrich Bonhoeffer's quote, "When Christ calls a man, he bids him come and die."[1] Dying is a process that holds within it a promise of new life as well. We are dying while waiting for Christ. We wait with the hungry and are fed; we shelter the homeless and find a home for ourselves and Christ amongst us; we take our breaths alongside those taking their last and find ourselves mysteriously breathing in the very life-giving breath of God. As we journey with those who see us as the "other" we are healed and touched by the "other" we welcome.

I don't know which choices will change the course of the life of the church in the twenty-first century. From century to century the church has changed. It is changing still; thank God for that grace. I recently read an

---

1. Bonhoeffer, *Cost of Discipleship*, 99.

article on the website Ministry Matters, written by Ron Edmonson offering his opinion to churches that are in need of revitalization in the midst of changing demographics. He offers three suggestions, either to reach out to those in the changing communities and "become like the community"; to "leave the community," that is relocate the church into another context that might bring in folks more like those within the current church; or to "slowly die in the community," that is let the church die.[2] When I share this article, the church folks just gaze back at me with sheep-like eyes, and with the same sheep-like eyes, I too gaze at the Good Shepherd.

Churches as communities of people connected to the church building in both nurturing and challenging ways have taught me to trust that God is with us in both the dying and the living, both physically and spiritually, both individually and as a community. I continue to wait, not passively but actively in prayer and discernment, doing small things with a small number of the faithful in the presence of a loving and gracious Shepherd still leading, still feeding, still with us and with others along this journey. Spirit of life, come. . . . Come, Spirit come.

Bibliography

Bonhoeffer, Dietrich. *The Cost of Discipleship*. New York: Macmillan, 1963.

Edmonson, Ron. "When Your Church Life No Longer Reflects the Community." *Ministry Matters*. http://www.ministrymatters.com/all/entry/6279/when-your-church-no-longer-reflects-the-community.

---

2. Edmonson, "When Your Church Life No Longer Reflects the Community."

15

Still in Church

—David Frost

As THE SON OF a Presbyterian minister, I grew up in the church, and actually for a time during my father's first call, I lived literally next to the church. From a very early age I had a desire to one day serve the Lord in a similar fashion as my father. However, as is often the case, life got in the way. So it was not until I was close to fifty years old that I attended New York Theological Seminary in pursuit of a Master of Divinity degree.

Up until that time I had served as a lay leader in the church and was engaged in various ministries involving both music and youth work. It was in that capacity that I believe I first was able to really hear the Spirit as it somehow found me in my discontent with the institutional church, speaking to me deeply through the voices of the youth I was working with.

I was always a good kid when it came to church. I supported my father in his ministry endeavors long after my siblings had left the church. But I was also restless deep within my spirit, needing more than just rote religion. After college, where I spent my time trying to craft my own religion out of pieces of various world philosophies and religions I had studied, I became involved in a born-again community in my hometown. However, that also would prove to be ultimately not enough to reconcile the image of God that was offered by fairly conservative Christianity with the uneasiness deep inside me. The God I yearned to believe in truly was a God of unconditional love, a very different image than anything being offered: a God of forgiveness and mercy, of unending love and patience, of grace and goodness in spite of my humanness. And so my pursuit of God continued, sometimes moving slightly towards more literal and traditional outlooks and other times going quite far in the opposite direction.

Through it all, I feel that God was incredibly faithful, letting me work it all out in my own time and in my own ways. In the end—or perhaps more accurately, in the beginning—I found myself leaning heavily on the Spirit of God as revealed within my own heart as my only trusted source of truth and authority. And while I understand that there are those who will say that such an approach is very risky due to a complete lack of checks or balances, I loved my Lord so deeply that I was willing to risk being wrong or misguided on occasion, if it meant I could be closer to the real source of love and of life.

So I guess it is not all that surprising that I developed a radical commitment to searching for and finding the place or places where the Spirit of God is at work in the world today, regardless of whether it was within or outside of traditional church walls, outside the building. I developed a commitment to listen to all voices willing to speak, and in particular to those not often allowed to express themselves in "proper" religious dialogue, especially the voices of today's young people. After many years of working within the literal walls of the faith, I still retain a deep commitment and willingness to place any and all things of belief and faith practice upon the altar of the Lord, to see whether or not it is still fresh and new, for I remain unafraid to look anew for that which is being called for by the Spirit of holiness in this time.

Along the way I found myself venturing quite far afield of traditional practices, experimenting with different styles of living and practicing faith. However, the slide away from tradition really began in earnest on the way home from a youth mission trip. We had stopped for a break and a debrief time at a rest stop on the thruway. We all grabbed a snack or coffee and gathered around at some tables outside. I asked the young people, who were mostly middle-school- or early-high-school-age, to reflect on the time they had just spent in service of others in need, as well as on how they felt about returning home and the re-entry into normal life. They all agreed that the experience had been deeply connecting for them in terms of seeing God as a real and living force at work in the lives of those they encountered that week. But they also expressed a level of sadness that they did not feel as though they would be able to worship as they had all week long upon returning home. Traditional liturgical expression did not hold their interest at all and they were saddened by the contrast between that and the worship experiences they had just left behind. During the week they had participated several times daily in experiential worship that included concrete testimony of what was perceived to be the actions of the Holy Spirit among them; contemporary music, the lyrics of which they were able to relate to; and hands-on reflection times that were multi-sensory and easy for them to access spiritually. It was these aspects of worship and of their faith experience that they expressed sadness at leaving behind.

As the youth leader of the church, I was struck by the young people's sincerity and openness and the way they expressed a desire to continue to worship upon returning home in a way that was meaningful to them. I conferred with the other youth leaders during the rest of the trip home and we decided right then and there to find a way to provide a worship experience for the youth that would be as meaningful as the one they had just left behind. We arrived back home on a Saturday evening and on Sunday night, the very next day, we began holding a second worship service that was similar to the ones the youth had found so meaningful the week before. We used the songs they had learned, we had time for sharing experiences of the Spirit in their lives, and we were sure to include a short reflection and meditation portion with a hands-on sensory element.

The Sunday night services were a huge hit with the youth who began to invite their friends to come and find out about this new way to find God in their lives. Others in the congregation heard about the alternative service as well and soon we had a large group of youth and adults attending regularly, so much so that Sunday morning attendance began to suffer dramatically. It was at this point that I realized that for the church to survive, I would need to find a way to bridge the gap between the traditional service and the new, more youth-accessible one. I asked the youth to carefully and prayerfully consider whether they would be willing to come back to worship on Sunday mornings if we were to change the content and experience of the morning service to be more in line with what they were used to. Reluctantly they said yes and we began the attempt to combine the two different styles and expectations into one worshipping unit.

Another force was working deeply on me at this time, as it was also the period when I was attending seminary several nights a week. At New York Theological Seminary I encountered a God I had never really known before. It was during these several years that I first heard the myriad gospel calls for justice within the framework of faith in action. Prior to that, I had focused mostly, if not exclusively, on both salvation and "how to get to heaven" faith practice, not hearing or knowing the Jesus who spoke deeply of the call to justice. However, having heard the call as I was seeking to deal with the merging of our two congregations into one gave me new insight as well as new passion for engaging people of all ages into a gospel message I finally could accept as my own.

And so we worked together for several years, finding new meaning and new purpose in a faith that truly was finally others-centered rather than just an individualistic pursuit of eternal reward. After graduating and being commissioned as pastor, I began to search even more deeply for meaning that would sustain this very mixed group of congregants. I decided to hold a series of Vision Quest meetings with any and all who were interested. Again, it was the young people who responded most enthusiastically. For in truth, the switch over to a mixed/hybrid service of both what they had experienced on Sunday nights and traditional liturgy did not really hold them as well as I had hoped.

However, they were still interested in pursuing this God we had so long been searching for. So, while there were several interested adults who attended the Vision Quest meetings, there were an equal number of youth who came to listen and give voice as well. Over the course of several months we all together came up with a wholly new plan to meld our newfound passion for community service along with more traditional faith practices. We introduced our ideas to the congregation in early 2010 and in April of that same year began to practice our every other week rotation between our hybrid traditional Sunday worship and what we called Service Sundays—Sundays set aside to worship through acts of outreach and community service, reconvening again for lunch before departing for the day. Prior to starting the new plan I circulated a letter to the congregation informing them of the new changes.

The letter read as follows:

> This is a proposal to start a new worship initiative that calls for us to spend every other Sunday morning in the active worship of community outreach and service. . . . Every other Sunday was selected as the time allotment to allow us to engage our current food pantry outreach in the project, allowing us to expand that effort with food drop-offs to shut-ins, as well as to offer the opportunity for those taking advantage of the food pantry program to share a common meal together with us on those Sunday afternoons.
>
> The four primary objectives of this initiative are: 1.) to allow us to worship together in alternative styles, worshipping with our whole bodies, with our hands and feet, gifts and talents, 2.) to enable us to deepen the interrelationships within the church family

through applied, cooperative service, 3.) to provide a visible and dynamic presence within our community, and 4) to allow us to reengage more of our youth in active Church participation.

It is anticipated that we will begin our "Service Sundays" at the same time as presently with Sunday School and Adult Bible Study from 8:45 to 9:30 a.m. and then assembly of all around 9:30 a.m. to divide up into service teams for the morning. The "service" time will begin with communal prayer after which groups will go out and serve until 11:45 a.m. or so at which time we will gather together for lunch in the Fellowship Hall. We will begin each lunch with a brief celebration of the Lord's Supper after which we will eat together and then depart. We anticipate opening this shared meal to the whole community including any who wish to join us from the Food Pantry.

To begin with, we will have a simple meal each time such as soup, homemade bread, and salad. The church will purchase supplies for this until such time that donations made at the lunch can offset the cost. As an alternative we may want to consider asking for volunteer families to take one Sunday a month to pay for the meal costs much like we did with the breakfasts.

There will be an occasional visitor to church who will be unprepared to participate in certain of the activities; however there will always be several areas in which they will be able to assist. To this end . . . it is important that we strive to make these folks welcome and comfortable, as well as to adequately publicize our schedule through appropriate sign announcements and word of mouth sharing.

The service teams were given the opportunity to rotate through various service opportunities: food pantry assistance, work on or around the church property, town flower barrel care, work on various projects around town, visits to shut-ins, nursing homes or other churches with a gift of music, meal preparation for the noon meal, and care for the church garden.

This move met with great success for quite some time, resulting in the church gaining favorable exposure both within the community as well as in the larger institutional church of which our church was a member. However, after a while I noticed that there were a number of members who only came for the short vesper service and did not participate in the rest of the Service Sunday activities. Upon questioning them as to how we might make it more to their liking, they told me that they had spent much of their lives involved in community service and really wanted to just come to church.

And so, after several years, I realized that the Service Sundays had pretty much run their course and that their season had come to an end. However, during that time we were also able to grow the congregation into a more diverse and viable group which enabled us to carry on in other, different ways of worshipping and living together as Christians. Ironically I suppose, after spending so much time actively seeking out new ways of being the church, we now are back within the sanctuary with a regular Sunday morning service once again. However, we are not the same church that worshiped within the walls when my father was the pastor.

Having spent so much time listening and seeking, we are now a very open and inclusive congregation, welcoming all who stop in and counting within our membership individuals of many different faith expressions including a number of former Roman Catholics. We meet in our old place with a new commitment to discerning how to best serve our community. We truly feel that it is our life together that binds and holds us together rather than some physical entity. And while the physical buildings we own are still a major focus of our concerns and a significant portion of our fiscal responsibility and activity, we see those buildings with new eyes—with eyes looking for ways in which to use them more fully, more responsibly, and more for the benefit of the community as a whole rather than as just for the congregation.

I think that most fellowshipping communities need some place in which they can gather and feel comfortable. They do not need to call it their own, but they do need a place to come together to share and to be renewed as they worship God and spend time together as family listening for the Spirit's guidance in how best to share the light and love of Christ to the community they call home.

I have also come to take a fairly practical view of the apparent demise of the institutional church over last several decades. I have watched it swing from left or center to far right. I also hold on to a view of a God who first left the church and then called from outside any who were willing to follow, any who were willing to look for those intersections of the holy, with life lived in the public square, and willing to look for ways to partner with other individuals and bodies of individuals to do the called work of the Spirit regardless of the spiritual orientation or lack thereof of those partners.

I wonder if Christianity has become so tainted with false images and understandings that it might be necessary for those who truly follow Jesus to do so almost in secret, letting their life lived out in the public square be their effective witness more so than their words of stated theology. There is today, perhaps more than ever before, an absolute need for a deep partnership with the Holy Spirit to sense where, when, and whom is the object of God's designs; to discover where and what is the point of need being shown to you, in order to find the courage and will to dwell therein and to give all you have been asked to in that place. Also, there still remains a need to have a place for those seeking God to assemble. Watchman Nee reminds us that it matters not where, but gathering is vital in order to wash the feet clean of the dust of daily life lived in service.

We need to find a balance between nostalgic love of the church of our fathers and mothers, and the always possible call to "come away" from that by the Spirit, in a search for new wineskins to hold the new wine of God's work, which is surely being fermented now. This is not necessarily a headlong rush away from the current residences we may have, but surely a willingness to see them as temporary residences that are there and deserve to be well-stewarded until such time that they no longer are needed (which requires a deep consideration of what "well-stewarded" means, for keeping, heating, and insuring a large sanctuary building merely for approximately fifty-two hours a year may not actually be holy use).

There is a notion that space—any space—is often viewed as something of value to someone. This needs to be contrasted with, or perhaps separated from, the idea that God is one to be feared if we do not set aside the best we have solely for adoration and worship alone, if we are ever going to get closer to a more human understanding of God with us and in us. This may require us to reimagine that all church buildings, whether they are used or owned by the church, must be fitted or retrofitted to allow for multiple uses and need to be used fully for the good of those served. This notion of 24/7 stewardship of church facilities is not just to support the church's ability to carry them, but also to provide space for others within the community.

However, these notions most often will not be accepted easily by traditional congregations. The strength of resistance to change may in fact be correlated to the length of time those using the building have been a part of that community, as well as how homogeneous the congregation is in terms of faith tradition origin. The more they are all alike, the more resistance is possible, leading to a call to validate individual freedom to worship and fellowship wherever they feel called and wherever they are fed.

It is also interesting to see what happens when long-departed, now freshly-back-in-the-faith individuals come back in, seeking to answer a call within to once again connect with the holy. It is equally fascinating to see how the church may have in fact changed dramatically in response to the Spirit's guidance during their time away. This may lead to a certain disconnect for those coming back expecting to find the church of their childhood or the church of their Sunday school memories. They may find instead a different fellowship in the old space which not only is totally different, but also places new demands upon them in the contemporary movement of faith's push towards more gospel-centered values of pursuing justice for those in the margins, of social outreach and activism, of contemporary worship styles, music, and liturgy (term used loosely). There can be confusion, due to the radically different church landscape of some newly Spirit-led fellowships, and this may cause difficulties in understanding and communication as the church continues to search for that new wine that is most assuredly calling for new wineskins.

We are brought back to the fact that the danger, or perhaps the opportunity, is that the new wine of the new church just may not fit well within the wineskins of large, old, mostly single-function, and expensive-to-keep church buildings. And yet, in many cases, congregations may not have a clear pathway that is viable to leave their current residence behind. The state of the economy along with actual architectural configurations will lead to many and varying models of potential building use. In our particular case, the facilities are burdensome, but we do not feel a consensus call to move on to somewhere else, for not only are they representative of a long-standing force and presence within our community, but they seem to be filled with potential, and capable of being re-purposed/re-imagined as multiple use "anchor facilities" within our local community.

This is not to say that we do not come up against a certain resistance to change or to use certain of the facilities in other ways. There are still passionate beliefs that sanctuaries should be spaces set aside solely for worship and that alone, and not as facilities that might otherwise house or even occasionally support secular pursuits such as youth activities, including concerts, parties, or sports; locations for farmer's markets, or indeed any money-making activities at all; dances; or other traditionally non-church functions. In some ways it seems that all of this comes down to a question as to the identity of the church. Is it a fellowship, a Spirit-led body seeking the guidance and favor of the Lord? Or is it an historically-based group, a denomination associated with a particular physical space?

We also need to consider the allure and relative value of the advertised connectionism of larger denominations. Perhaps we need to severely downsize larger associations' presence, and frankly the cost to the local church. This means insisting that the larger, institutional church make a commitment to provide only that which is truly beneficial. The institutional church or denomination needs to let go of its drive for self-preservation and insistence upon ordering itself by "Robert's most annoying rules of human life." Instead, the institutional church could effectively focus on communicating that which is working, sharing the movement of the Spirit wherever it touches down among us. Thus the larger church body would be something it was in the early days of Christianity, a truly catholic body, gathering up and then sharing new life with smaller, local church communities. This is, I believe, the real mission of the larger church if indeed there is one, a mission most ancient and at the same time new.

I honestly feel that the church will survive and address whatever need presents itself, for in some way churches reflect the tenor of human life. Many flock to communities that speak well of their core beliefs across the full bandwidth of liberal to conservative expression. Currently, the right-leaning tendencies of white culture support older, regimented forms of expression. There is genuine fear of what is new or different, just as there is fear, even loathing of those who are other, different. We find more progressive expressions at the margins of white privilege and culture among people of color, immigrants, those of lower income, and of less traditional religious belonging and expression. Among such Americans, cultural expression and inclusivity tend to be vibrant, but have fewer financial resources. Though their practice seems more experimental, it seems better able to reach and impact the lives of those who truly are unchurched, or who have turned away from or left the church. Traditional, conservative churches seem more intent on serving churched but disaffected individuals instead, taking new members from other Christian traditions rather that the ranks of the unchurched.

To conclude, in many ways we have left our traditional understanding and trappings of church and walked boldly out in search of what God is doing outside the walls. Maybe it is not so much that "the church has left the building," really, as much as the building no longer defines church. We have found much in the way of new wine as well as a deeper understanding of why we chose to live as people of faith. And, while we came back within the walls, we are no longer the same people as before. We came back into a place that was comfortable and renewing. But at the same time, we are a people listening for the Spirit's call. Our leadership, we hope, is more than willing to go wherever we feel that call asks us to go. The future is unknown, but our guide and friend Jesus Christ is not. *Soli Deo Gloria.*

16

Many Mansions:
Reimagining the Church and
Its Buildings in the Global City

—Kenneth J. Guest

As THE NEW YORK City weather grew colder in September of 2011, the protesters of Occupy Wall Street began to look for shelter from the elements at night. The Church of St. Paul and St. Andrew United Methodist in Manhattan was one of a handful of congregations to open its doors to Occupiers from across the country. Each night for over a month, more than one hundred Occupiers converged on the church after full days of demonstrating against inequality in the global economy. Sleeping bags and blankets were strewn across the cavernous sanctuary. Small groups formed to discuss the day, the police, and the economy. And every morning the Occupiers would rise, gather their belongings, and head back downtown to Wall Street to continue their protests.

As they left the church building at the crack of dawn there was no reason to exit quietly. The church—as it is everyday—was already bustling. At 6 A.M. cooks arrive to prepare five hundred meals for seniors in the neighborhood through a Meals on Wheels program. Food delivery trucks pass waiting customers of the West Side Campaign Against Hunger, New York City's largest emergency food pantry, as its fifty staff and volunteers prepare to feed and counsel the 250 families that arrive daily. At the same time, ten women in the overnight women's shelter sponsored by the church and sister synagogue Congregation B'nai Jeshurun were showering and breakfasting before heading out to look for work—all of this before 7 A.M. each morning. On any given day, the church operates 24/7: children's community music classes, a Spanish-language preschool, cooking classes, exercise

133

classes, high school and community orchestras, a theater production, a Jewish Torah study group, an after-school tutoring program mobilizing volunteers to work with seventy local school children and their parents, cooking for young women transitioning out of New York's sex trade, an African-American LGBTQ church choir rehearsal, and church committee meetings. All of this by the time the protesters from occupy Wall Street would return for their evening of rest and warmth each night.

This church has definitely not left the building. But it has left behind an older way of being the church and reimagined itself in today's most vibrant global city. And it has taught many of us about community, love, and the power of collective action.

The Church and the City

St. Paul and St. Andrew's history intimately intersects the history of New York City. As Manhattan's Five Points and Lower East Side neighborhoods were being settled by immigrants from England, Ireland, Germany, and China, as well as freed African slaves, the original congregation was established in 1835 on Mulberry Street on Manhattan's Lower East Side as the Second Wesleyan Chapel (later renamed the Mulberry Street Methodist Episcopal Church) and engaged in ministries with the poor, particularly vulnerable immigrant women and children served by the Methodist Five Points Mission. The congregation, renamed St. Paul's Methodist Episcopal Church, later moved uptown to Twenty-Second Street and Fourth Avenue in 1857 to the heart of the city's roiling garment district bursting with immigrant workers toiling in hundreds of overcrowded and dangerous sweatshops. A gift of industrialist, financier, and member Daniel Drew, the white marble church with a 210-foot spire became known as "the cathedral church of Methodism," and served as a site of crucial debates about slavery and the Civil War.

The congregation next relocated to its current location in the bucolic farmland, rolling hills, and streams of Manhattan's Upper West Side that were being settled as the city's population expanded northward. The eclectic, asymmetrical limestone and terracotta twin-steepled edifice opened in 1897. St. Paul's leadership built a tall-steepled church to attract fine preachers and a well-heeled membership that arrived in carriages (and later limousines) to be greeted by white-gloved ushers in evening jackets. The sanctuary ceiling soared upward five stories. Three dropped chandeliers illuminated seating for twelve hundred on the main floor and a vast U-shaped balcony. The organ sounded four thousand separate pipes. An attached education wing was appointed with wood-framed, high-ceilinged parlors, chapel, a three-story concert hall, and classrooms. In 1937 St. Paul's merged with struggling nearby St. Andrews congregation. Methodists filled the sanctuary on the corner of Eighty-Sixth Street well into the 1950s.

The 1960s, however, brought an abrupt decline in the economic and social conditions of Manhattan's Upper West Side, and New York City itself, which would last for over twenty years and reshape the congregation in the process. Deindustrialization hammered working class residents as corporations relocated jobs and factories, first to the South and then overseas to lower costs and increase profits. A global recession and oil crisis rocked the world economy. A dramatic disinvestment in urban areas by the federal government under the Nixon administration left New York City pouring far more into the national tax pool than it was receiving in federal government support. By the mid 1970s, basic city services of fire, police, and sanitation were severely curtailed. Fires raged through sections of the Bronx as landlords abandoned buildings and set them on fire to collect the insurance payments. Middle-class residents began leaving a city in decline. The city's fiscal free fall left it teetering on the verge of bankruptcy. A famous *New York Post* headline in October of 1975, reflecting the Federal government's unwillingness to assist a wounded city, read "Ford to City: Drop Dead."

St. Paul and St. Andrew's foundations were also rocked by these changes. White middle-class residents fled to the suburbs, emptying the neighborhood and leaving behind the elderly and the poor. Homelessness, which had not been a significant problem before the 1975 fiscal crisis, exploded. Members of the city's expanding Hispanic immigrant population replaced the departing middle class and well-off apartment dwellers. Church membership declined precipitously throughout this period, its demographic shifts mapping changes in the surrounding neighborhood. With few cash reserves and a collapsing financial base, the congregation struggled to maintain an aging and rapidly deteriorating building. A self-study led by a leading team of United Methodist church planners assessed the congregation's prospects. Their findings suggested the church had less than two years to survive and recommended closure and sale of the property. Would the church leave the building? There was strong incentive to move in that direction.

Whither the Building?

With little hope of maintaining the aging building, but a stubborn desire to remain in the neighborhood, in 1975 the congregation convened a Church Committee on Future Alternatives to consider its options. Interviews conducted with church members active during that time suggest that two different yet eventually-intersecting visions began to emerge out of this moment of crisis. Some key leaders began to explore options to leverage the value of the church's land to secure the future. Specifically they hoped to find a developer who would lease the underlying property, demolish the current church structure, and erect a luxury high-rise residential tower where the church now stood. In return, new church facilities would be built in the cellar and first two floors, and the congregation would receive a cash payment to support its ongoing work. The congregation voted in 1979 to demolish the building. But as word of the development plan leaked into the surrounding community, a group of neighbors in adjoining buildings mobilized a petition to have the church designated a historical landmark by the city. With the tragic demolition of New York's Penn Station in 1964 and the near loss of Grand Central Station to developers, New York had implemented a series of landmarks laws designed to aid in the preservation of buildings of historical significance. But by the 1970s, neighborhood groups were beginning to wield these laws to deter demolition and redevelopment of far less monumental properties. St. Paul and St. Andrew became a target of this movement. In November of 1981 the New York City Landmark's Commission officially designated the church a historical landmark against the congregation's wishes. The designation required the congregation to maintain the exterior of the building unchanged, at the congregation's expense.

At the same time as these more formal deliberations about the property were being engaged, others in the congregation turned outward to focus on addressing the burgeoning needs of the community that was being devastated by the city's economic decline. How could the church serve the needs of its neighbors? They also turned to the building as a resource. In 1974 the church sexton and other members opened a small on-site senior lunch program in the church basement to serve elderly people left behind in the mass exodus to the suburbs. By the 1980s the program had grown into a full Meals on Wheels project, preparing and delivering up to five hundred meals, six days a week. In 1978 the congregation, together with representatives of neighboring churches and synagogues, organized an ecumenical conference on hunger on the West Side of Manhattan. In 1979 the West Side Campaign Against Hunger (WSCAH) was formed to provide emergency food assistance to those in the neighborhood who could not make ends meet. Initially operated out of a third floor closet in the church, today WSCAH is the city's largest and most innovative emergency food pantry, serving 250 families a day, providing social service counseling to all customers, and modeling a customer-based, supermarket-style pantry being replicated across the country. Also in 1979, the congregation launched a ministry to college students in the Columbia University area that quickly expanded in the early 1980s to include young adults and a Christian Artists Fellowship.

The empty spaces of the church building began to fill with people—with needs, with possibilities, and with imaginations. What would the future hold for this building and these people? Could the congregation synthesize two emerging visions and strategies? Would the congregation even survive long enough to find out?

My Journey with the Church

I arrived in New York City—and at St. Paul and St. Andrew—in August 1981 to attend Columbia University as both the city and the church were deep in the process of reimagining themselves and their future. My first Sunday in New York, with the whole city at my fingertips, I looked up local United Methodist churches. Force of habit for the son of a United Methodist minister? Loneliness in a strange city? I hopped the number one subway train from Columbia's 116th Street stop to Eighty-Sixth Street. Sure, my first-year orientation program had warned me about the dangerous and deteriorated neighborhoods just south of campus. But I was completely naïve to the crises that were reshaping the city. Nor did I imagine the struggles of most of the city's Protestant churches in those changing times.

Thinking I was headed for a big New York City United Methodist congregation, I went early to get a good seat. To my surprise, I walked into a dimly lit, cavernous, empty space at 10:45 that morning. By 11 A.M., when worship was scheduled to start, there were perhaps fifteen people. I was befuddled. Mysteriously, with no apparent human intervention, the organ began to play. Two black-robed clergymen entered from a side door to the chancel area, bowed at the altar and took seats hidden behind the large elevated lectern and pulpit. From their perches, they took turns rising, turning on small lamps, reading a scripture or prayer over a crackling old sound system, turning off the lamps and sitting down. The organ played. A choir of five sang. I struggled to see through the seeming midday dusk. I thought to myself, "Well, the church has certainly left this old building!" But I was wrong.

Thirty-five years later I still call St. Paul and St. Andrew my church home. Walking back up Broadway to my Columbia dorm that August Sunday in 1981, I had no way of knowing what a formative and foundational role St. Paul and St. Andrew would play in the next thirty-five years of my life. Nor could I see the rebirth and rejuvenation of this urban congregation that would unfold in the years to come and that I would have the privilege of being a part of. What appeared for all intents and purposes to be a dying congregation strung together by a wish and a prayer, held within it the seeds of rebirth and revitalization. And as the church reinvented itself, it taught me about being the church, and provided me a place to put to work my deep commitments to the welfare of all humanity and the potential for building a more intentional and life-giving human community. For where a dwindling and aging congregation struggled to imagine a way forward in a city shattered by globalization, deindustrialization, white flight, and disinvestment, they had the courage to respond to the needs of neighbors for food, hospitality, community, and hope far beyond the congregation's capacity to meet, and the desire to remain rooted in that community. This is what nurtured a spark strong enough to rekindle a vision and sense of purpose and mission. On that first Sunday in 1981 I could not see that the very building, which appeared dead, and which I know now had come to feel to many like an albatross weighing the congregation to the bottom of the sea, held in its very complexity and neediness the possibility of reimagining what a relevant and vital church could look like in twenty-first-century New York.

In the ensuing years the congregation continued to explore its vision and mission. With no resources to fulfill the Landmark Commission's mandate to preserve the building's exterior, and no funding from the city, in the 1980s church leaders began a decade-long, but ultimately unsuccessful, battle to have the landmark designation removed. Both administrative and first-amendment remedies proved unsuccessful. But the congregation continued to explore ways to respond to the needs of the neighborhood. In 1985 the congregation opened a nightly homeless shelter for women staffed by church volunteers. In 1989 the congregation voted to become one of the first United Methodist reconciling congregations, openly welcoming lesbian and gay members and advocating for equal rights within the church and society. In 1990 the church began to partner with the conservative Jewish synagogue, Congregation B'nai Jeshurun, engaging in interfaith dialogue and action, and attempting to model in a racially- and religiously-divided city new ways of living and working together across barriers that have historically separated. In 1991, seeking a synthesis of the many strong visions that had emerged, the congregation voted to seek its future through the development of an interfaith and interchurch center, a vision that has developed over twenty-five years in the existing property, rather than a new construction.

An Anthropologist's Theological Reflection on Church Buildings

"In my Father's house there are many dwelling places," Jesus said to his disciples gathered in Jerusalem for Passover shortly before his arrest, crucifixion, and resurrection (John 14:2) As an anthropologist now, I have become curious about this phrase. What would it have meant to Jesus, an illiterate Mediterranean Jewish peasant living under Roman occupation in first-century Israel and preaching and living a message of free eating, free healing, intentional community, and non-violent action to bring about the reign of God? What does it mean for people of faith wrestling with aging buildings and seeking a renewed sense of mission and vision? "In my Father's house there are many dwelling places," he is quoted by the author of John to have said to his disciples as they gathered in Jerusalem and as he tried to explain his impending death to them. "I go to prepare a place for you."

In the ancient Mediterranean Middle East of this time, the image of the household would have resonated for Jesus and his followers on multiple levels. Jesus—son of a carpenter and most likely a carpenter himself—would have understood what it took to build a house. The rank of carpenter was not that of a skilled tradesman or artisan as we might think of it today. Rather, carpenters were a rank below the landed peasants, a part of the landless poor who would not have had a household of their own. And so the image of the household would have had powerful ideological resonance as he spoke to the poor, oppressed, and marginalized in Israel. The phrase "in my father's house" would have evoked a powerful image of kinship, belonging, home, place, the extended family of multiple generations and marriages living together—parents, sons and wives, children and grand-children—an image Jesus refers to frequently as the kingdom of God.

In the Gospels we meet Jesus as a mendicant prophet, calling forth a radical people's movement based on a commitment to free feeding for all (feeding the five thousand, turning water into wine at the wedding at Cana, eating with Pharisees and tax collectors: "I am the bread of life. Whoever comes to me will never be hungry, and whoever believes in me will never be thirsty" [John 6:35]); free healing for all, regardless of race, ethnicity, class, social position (the lame man at the pool at the Sheep's Gate, the blind beggar's eyes healed with a mixture of mud and saliva—all on the Sabbath); radical community of shared possessions and a common purse—all built on the revolutionary commandment to love, not a call to political or military revolution against the religious authorities (see: Pharisees), local politicians (see: Pontius Pilate), or Roman occupiers (see: Caesar). Certainly there were others making that claim for violent revolution and change. But Jesus envisioned a movement based instead on radical acts of love and inclusion.

It is in this context that we must consider Jesus' image of "my father's house." In it, says Jesus, there are many dwelling places. In Greek, the word so often translated as "mansions" literally means "dwelling places, dwell-ings, resting places, rooms, abodes." In patriarchal Mediterranean culture, rooms would have been added to the household as the family grew through birth or marriage. In a household with many dwelling places, there would be shelter for all, room for all, no danger of overcrowding. And there they would find welcome, safety, food, and family. What would it mean for a Christian congregation today to attempt to create that vision of a place of God with many mansions—many dwelling places in which the family would find food, shelter, and love?

In the midst of the social upheaval and congregational decline, the Church of St. Paul and St. Andrew planted the seeds of its restoration—not in a church that left the building but in a church that reclaimed the build-ing, reimagined the building, and believed that in God's house there could be many mansions, places of safety and dwelling and feeding and healing for all members of the family of God.

Radical feeding. It began with a small food pantry and a third floor closet stocked with parishioners' donated canned foods. It started with an idea that some older people in the neighborhood, left behind as their children fled the city in the 1970s, needed a place to have lunch and talk together. *Radical hospitality*. It began as a wishful response to house the growing number of homeless people sleeping on the church's steps. It started with a few kids needing help with their homework. *Radical inclusiveness*. It started because two rabbis and two pastors wanted to learn from each other and model for their congregations, their city, and world how people of different faiths might live and work together. It started with the belief that LGBTQ people are without question a part of the household of God and church members marching in the Gay Pride Parade singing Jesus Loves Me, This I Know. And it began with a creative determination to see how the assets bequeathed by a previous generation could be put to work in new ways by a succeeding generation. In my Parent's house are many mansions.

My journey and the journey of St. Paul and St. Andrew have been deeply interwoven over the past thirty-five years. I was drawn in by its fledgling campus ministry program and those young people, many still active in the church, who were seriously exploring the intersections of faith and life. I was drawn in to its engagement with the social gospel—a deep, faith-based involvement in the work of social justice in the local community. I was drawn to its sense of global engagement. "The world is my parish," said Methodism's founder John Wesley. And I was exploring my sense of being a global citizen, to see the world more completely, consciously, and awake. Perhaps most significantly, I was drawn to the possibility of building an authentic community of friends and fellow travellers with whom I could share a life-long journey to understand my place and purpose in the world and work together to make the world a better place.

Throughout my journeys—student, China scholar, church worker, anthropologist, and author—the church has been a touchstone. And in its journey of growth and renewal I have been inspired on my own way.

Lightning Source UK Ltd.
Milton Keynes UK
UKOW03f1943100517

300931UK00002B/177/P